BASEBALL IN
TACOMA-PIERCE
COUNTY

A large crowd gathered outside the News Tribune Building to watch the box score for game four of the World Series between the Philadelphia Athletics and the St. Louis Cardinals on October 5, 1930. Although Cardinals pitcher Jesse Haines outdueled Lefty Grove, 3-1, to tie the Series up at two wins apiece, the Athletics would ultimately prevail, winning the World Series four games to two. (Courtesy Tacoma Public Library, Bowen collection.)

FRONT COVER: Cy Greenlaw (left) and cousin Earl Kuper were teammates for the Tacoma Tigers of the Western International League during the 1946 and 1947 seasons.

COVER BACKGROUND: The Amocats (Tacoma spelled backwards) fielded a team from 1901 to 1906.

BACK COVER: Teams march into Athletic Park at Fourteenth and Sprague Streets for opening day of the City League season in 1915.

BASEBALL IN TACOMA-PIERCE COUNTY

Marc H. Blau

ARCADIA
PUBLISHING

Published by Arcadia Publishing
Charleston, South Carolina

Printed in the United States of America

Library of Congress Control Number: 2010932848

For all general information, please contact Arcadia Publishing:
Telephone 843-853-2070
Fax 843-853-0044
E-mail sales@arcadiapublishing.com
For customer service and orders:
Toll-Free 1-888-313-2665

Visit us on the Internet at www.arcadiapublishing.com

To Clay Huntington, a dear friend and walking almanac of local sports history; baseball and softball old-timers everywhere; and to my wife, Cheryl; my children, CJ and Chad; and my parents, Kurt and May Blau.

CONTENTS

ACKNOWLEDGMENTS

I would like to thank every baseball and softball player, coach, umpire, administrator, broadcaster, sportswriter, team physician, trainer, batboy, and groundskeeper that I have visited with over the past 25 years. Their amazing stories are inspiring, and without their willingness to share photographs and memories this book would not be possible.

Clay Huntington, a longtime broadcaster, radio station owner, and sports fan and historian, has encouraged and fueled my passion of local sports. From taking me into the clubhouse at Cheney Stadium at age 11 to get Willie Mays's and Juan Marichal's autographs, to enjoying our 1989 World Series trip, he is a great friend and one that I admire and respect.

The contributions to baseball in our community by Doug McArthur and Stan Naccarato are immeasurable as players, coaches, sponsors, broadcasters, administrators, and even umpires. Their efforts, combined with those of Clay and the generosity and passion for baseball shown by Ben Cheney, shaped the landscape for the national pastime in our backyard. We cannot thank them enough.

I am truly indebted to Jim Price, a former sports reporter for the Spokane *Spokesman-Review* and baseball historian extraordinaire, who offered considerable insights and stories for this book. David Eskenazi, whose dedication to preserving the history of baseball in Seattle, as well as the Pacific Coast League and Pacific Northwest, is unparalleled. Equally amazing is his incredible collection of photographs and recall about players and teams. Both Jim and David deserve significant credit for the success of this book. And, I would also like to acknowledge Eric Sallee, one of the creative forces, along with Jim and David, behind the book *Rain Check: Baseball in the Pacific Northwest*.

Other individuals who have volunteered with research, stories and/or loaned photographs from their personal collections include Kevin Kalal, Frank Colarusso, and Michael Sage. Thanks also go to John Wohn for scanning over 400 photographs to choose from; Jody Gomez and Marilyn Buri of the Artco Craft & Frame Shop; Dale Phelps and John McGrath of *The News Tribune* for their continued support in promoting our sports heritage; Ray Nemec for his treasure trove of statistical data for players; Brian Kamens, Bob Schuler, and Jody Gripp, the incredible staff in the Northwest Room at the Tacoma Public Library; and to the Tacoma Rainiers Baseball Club for their support.

The community owes a debt of gratitude to Baseball Tacoma Inc. for saving baseball from leaving Tacoma in the fall of 1971. Those individuals include original members Stan Naccarato, Robert Alessandro, Tom Baker, Dr. James Billingsley, Mike Block, Morley Brotman, Francis Browne, Ray Carlson, Lawrence Ghilarducci Sr., Doug Gonyea, Clay Huntington, Dr. Robert Johnson, Frank Manley, Carl Miraldi, Frank Pupo, Frank Ruffo, Jim Topping, Mike Tucci Sr., Walt Wiklund, Alden Woodworth, and E. J. "Jimmy" Zarelli. Joining later were Brad Cheney, Warren Chinn, Norma Honeysett, Robert Kelly, Gus Paine, Tom Paine, Mike Tucci Jr., and John Xitco.

Conspicuously missing from this book is the history of high school baseball due to space limitations and I would like to convey my apologies in that regard. Coaches such as Bill Mullen, Marv Scott, John Heinrick, Holly Gee, Merle Hagbo, Ed Hardenbrook, Marco Malich, Bob Lightfoot, Larry Marshall, and Andy Helling and players such as Harry Nygard, Bill Hobert, Gary Moore, Pat Rooney, Bill Parker, Joe Keller, and Phil Westendorf are among the cast of thousands that have graced the high school diamonds over the years and are deserving of recognition.

Finally, unless otherwise noted, all images appear courtesy of the author.

INTRODUCTION

Baseball fans in Tacoma-Pierce County are fortunate to have had the "national pastime" around for over 100 years. Since the first documented game in Tacoma, August 20, 1874, involving the Tacoma Invincibles, to the present, much has changed significantly—ballparks, equipment, the athleticism of players, coaching philosophies, and even strike zones. What has not changed, however, is the passion for the sport passed down from generation to generation. With the Tacoma Rainiers setting an all-time attendance record at Cheney Stadium in 2010, it is obvious that we have a good thing going on in our backyard. Well, here is a news flash—it's about to get better.

Even though my dad was born in Vienna, Austria, and knew nothing about the game of baseball, he still took me to my first game at Cheney Stadium in 1960; thus started my love affair with the Tacoma Giants. I worshipped Juan Marichal, Gil Garrido, and Gaylord Perry while listening to Don Hill's radio broadcasts and his signature call, " How about *that*, Giants fans?"

My hero, however, was Dusty Rhodes. Of course, at age nine I thought he was on his way up to the major leagues. How was I to know that he had been a World Series hero for the 1954 New York Giants and his career was on the downhill slide? That did not matter when 43 years later, I visited Dusty at his home in the Las Vegas area. I was still that little kid awed in the presence of my hero. It was everything I had ever dreamed of and more. We remained friends, and my most prized possession is his Pacific Coast League championship ring awarded to the 1961 Tacoma Giants.

Bob Maguinez, a household name in baseball circles in Tacoma as a player, umpire, scout, and administrator, and former Tacoma Giants pitcher John Pregenzer tried for five years to convince me to attend the annual Tacoma-Pierce County Baseball-Softball Old-Timers banquet. I resisted, asking them, "Why would I want to listen to a bunch of old codgers tell stories of their heydays?" When I finally relented, I was fascinated by the tales, mesmerized by the reverence placed upon certain players, impressed with the high esteem they felt about specific coaches, and entertained by the antics of umpires they fondly remembered. I was hooked.

Baseball and softball players, coaches, and umpires love to talk—A lot! Whether it was a 30-game season or a 162-game season, a great deal of time was spent together on the road or at home. Strong bonds of friendship were formed through these shared experiences.

Fortunately, I love to talk and listen, so I started conducting interviews on a regular basis. As stories were recorded, my archive of photographs, uniforms, bats, balls, and old baseball gloves grew, documenting the progression of baseball in our community.

Now a multi-million dollar industry, baseball has come a long way from local sandlots to the Eleventh Street Grounds, Athletic Park, Tiger Park, and finally Cheney Stadium. And thanks to the Schlegel Sports Group, along with a commitment from the City of Tacoma and a $5 million grant from the Ben B. Cheney Foundation under the leadership of Ben's children, Brad and Piper, Tacoma will enjoy a state-of-the-art $30 million remodeled ballpark in April, 2011.

As Al Gallagher, former Tacoma Giants and Cubs player said, "There are three things in my life which I really love: God, my family, and baseball. The only problem—once baseball season starts, I change the order around a bit."

See you at Cheney Stadium soon!

ABOUT THE ORGANIZATION

There are four organizations that have devoted considerable time and resources to the preservation of sports in Tacoma-Pierce County through written and visual mediums, and it is appropriate that these groups be recognized for their contributions in that regard.

Established in 1943 as a civic organization in Tacoma and Pierce County, the Tacoma Athletic Commission originally was formed as the Tacoma War Athletic Commission. Its purpose was to raise funds for athletic opportunities at nearby Fort Lewis and McChord Air Force Base during World War II.

The TAC has generated nearly $6 million to assist amateur athletic programs and athletes in Pierce County—not bad for a group whose first venture was a basketball game between Fort Lewis and the Harlem Globetrotters, played in the Tacoma Armory, where admission was 85¢.

Dedicated to sports and civic betterment, the TAC has been a leader in preserving the history of sports locally. In 1994, the TAC was instrumental in the creation of the Shanaman Sports Museum, which was established to preserve the community's sports heritage. Located at the Tacoma Dome, the museum archives significant images and artifacts used in this book.

In 2005, the TAC unveiled the book *Playgrounds to the Pros*, which captures the history of over 35 sports in the community from their inception through 2004. This was a significant contribution and indicative of the commitment to honor individuals and recognize their athletic achievements.

The Tacoma Athletic Commission also initiated the Tacoma-Pierce County Sports Hall of Fame in 1957 and was the driving force behind the State of Washington Sports Hall of Fame, created in 1960. Both were the brainchild of Clay Huntington, a founding member of the TAC.

Perhaps the most significant organization under the TAC's umbrella related to baseball is the Tacoma-Pierce County Baseball-Softball Old-Timers Association, which has been hosting banquets since the early 1950s. The group is dedicated to recognizing and honoring the many players, coaches, umpires, administrators, and teams that have been instrumental in the growth of baseball and softball in this community over the years. The Old-Timers Association has effectively helped maintain a connection to the past while documenting vital biographical information and preserving photographs.

Tacoma Athletic Commission	www.tacomaathletic.com
Shanaman Sports Museum	www.tacomasportsmuseum.com
TPC Baseball-Softball Old-Timers	www.oldtimerbaseball.com
State of Washington Sports Hall of Fame	www.washingtonsportshof.com

A M A T E U R   A N D
S E M I - P R O   B A S E B A L L
1 8 7 4 – 1 9 9 7

The reign of the Tacoma Invincibles, who were organized on August 8, 1874, was short lived as they played their first and last game 12 days apart. Yet the development of a baseball field at Eleventh and L Streets by John S. Baker in 1885 provided the impetus for the formation of countless amateur and semi-professional baseball teams throughout Pierce County.

Teams sprang up all over the city and one of the most memorable was the Amocats (Tacoma spelled backwards), who existed from 1901 to 1906. Leagues were organized based on the community a person lived in, ethnicity, and business, and so teams played in the Timber, Sunset, Valley, Commercial, Industrial, Twilight, Shipbuilders and City leagues among others.

The loose league affiliation did not prevent the South Tacoma Tigers from representing the West Coast in the Amateur Baseball Championship of the World in 1915 with their runner-up finish. It was not until 1937 that another Tacoma team ventured into postseason play, as the Johnson Paint team traveled to Wichita, Kansas, to compete in the National Baseball Congress tournament where they tied for fifth.

The Tacoma City League, resurrected in 1949, was the catalyst for a rebirth of baseball in the area, as community teams emerged in South Tacoma, Kay Street, Twenty-sixth and Proctor Streets, McKinley Hill, Sixth Avenue, and Thirty-eighth Street. The competition was fierce, and the crowds turned out in record numbers for games on neighborhood fields and at Tiger Park, located at Thirty-eighth and Lawrence Streets.

The formation of Stanley's Shoemen in 1955 resulted in epic battles against Tacoma's Woodworth Contractors for local supremacy, and in 1956 Stanley's claimed top honors with their American Amateur Baseball Congress National Championship. Woodworth would go on to be the runner-up in 1958. Thirty-eight years later, in 1996, the Tacoma Timbers took second place in the National Baseball Congress (semi-pro) World Series in Wichita, Kansas—the last national appearance by an area team.

Memories and legends were made on the field during these years of Tacoma baseball. Among the greats were Lou Balsano, George Wise, Al Pentecost, Ocky Haugland, Allan Browne, Sammy Cappa, Floyd "Lefty" Isekite, Frank Ruffo, Sonny Bailey, Cy Greenlaw, Morry Abbott, Earl Kuper, Dick Greco, Pete Sabutis, Cliff Schiesz, Jack Johnson, Dale Bloom, Mike Dillon, Earl Hyder, Bob Maguinez, George Grant, umpire Clarence Stave, and coaches John Heinrick, Marv Scott, and Doug McArthur, who head a cast of thousands. Here is a look.

The earliest documented photograph of a baseball game is shown here as the Leans defeated the Fats 24-17 on June 6, 1891, at the Orting Baseball Park in one of the most widely attended games of the season. (Washington State Historical Society, Tacoma.)

The Tacoma Athletic Club participated in the Pacific Northwest Amateur Baseball League, and its entry finished third with a 3-3 record against three other teams. The team played its games at the Eleventh Street Grounds and "the young men wear red perspirers," wrote the *Daily Ledger.*

AMATEUR AND SEMI-PRO BASEBALL: 1874–1997

The 1903 Tacoma Amateurs are, from left to right, (first row) Ed Hall, Glenn Matthews, and Elmer Gibbs; (second row) Ralph Votaw, Lind Messinger, Chet Strayer, ? Case, Fremont "Goo" Campbell Jr., and Joe Dickson; (third row) Leo Teats, Frank Hollis, and Ed Corey.

Captain Ed Corey led the Tacoma Cubs, and Clarence "Duke" Campbell managed them. The club played in an amateur league in 1904, and several of the players were also on the Tacoma Amateurs the previous season. Newspaper accounts indicate that in May, the Cubs faced the Amocats for the amateur league championship.

The Amocats (Tacoma spelled backwards) were formed in 1901, one year before the West Coast Grocery Company adopted the same name for its specially packed goods such as coffee and spices. Their last season was 1906, when they finished with a 24-3 record. Pictured here from left to right (front row) are Ralph Votaw, Glenn Matthews Jr., Ralph Teats, George Gates, and Fremont "Goo" Campbell Jr.; (second row) James "Spec" Gray, Clarence "Duke" Campbell, Frank Leslie, Andy Anderson, Pete Nicholson, and Roscoe Teats.

The Amocats defeated the Rainiers at Seattle's Madison Park on May 6, 1906, by a score of 14-7. According to a *Seattle Times* account, "The Rainiers were badly shot to pieces and the strong team from Tacoma simply trampled them in the dust of defeat." Pitcher "Duke" Campbell went on to become the auditor for Pierce County, and local folklore was that brother "Goo" was noted for being the only player in local history to knock in two runs with a three-base bunt.

During the 1909 season, Ed Hall (third row, far left) and brothers Clarence "Duke" Campbell (third row, middle), Fremont "Goo" Campbell Jr. (second row, far right), and Frank Cozza (first row, second from left) played for the Albers Brothers' Mush and Milk team in the News Commercial League sponsored by the *Daily News*. "Violet Oats" was the brand name for Albers Brothers products that opened in Tacoma in 1905.

The Pioneer Bindery and Printing Company baseball team poses with their trophy around 1911. Two members of the team included Jack Clark (second row, second from right) and Ed Hall (second row, far right). Ed played for the Amocats in 1906 and the Albers Brothers team in 1909, and his son Harry Hall played in the Shipbuilders League in the 1940s in Tacoma. Harry's nephew Bert Hall, a pitcher on the 1908 Tacoma Tigers Northwest League entry, was considered by some to be the originator of the forkball. (Tacoma Public Library.)

The 1912 Brewers were sponsored by the Pacific Brewery and played in the Tribune Twilight League against the Tacoma Grays, Pfisters, Dryers, the Courthouse, and the East Side Athletic Club. Games were played on the campus grounds of the College of Puget Sound. Two key players were Roy Wilkowski (first row, far left) and Allan Browne (first row, second from right). A right-handed shortstop who hit left-handed and had exceptional speed, "Brownie" also played for Hunt Mottet, the Olympic Club, Sixth Avenue, and the South Tacoma Tigers.

The Tacoma City League was formed in 1914, ran continuously until 1938, and then re-emerged in the late 1940s. The team sponsors reflected Tacoma of the past with well-known businesses sponsoring teams such as Superior Dairy, Olympic Ice Cream, Cammarano Brothers, Publix Garage, Kimball's, Model Lumber Company, and Johnson Paint. Often times communities were represented as well, such as Kay Street, Tacoma Avenue, Fern Hill, Sixth Avenue, McKinley Avenue, and Twenty-Third Street.

TACOMA CITY BASEBALL LEAGUE
PLAYER'S CONTRACT

I _Joseph Panowich_ hereby agree

to play with the _Oakland_ Baseball Club

in all scheduled games of the TACOMA CITY BASEBALL LEAGUE during the season of 1915.

Attest:

Oakland Baseball Club.   Signed _Joe. Penowich._ Player.

By _Leon Keirstead_ Manager.

The above contract becomes void when a player is released and he may be signed by another club after his release has been recognized by the president of the league.

Joe Penowich signed a contract to play in 1915 for manager Leon Keirstead of the Oakland Athletic Club in the City League. A series of regulations governing the league included the following: (1) players must be residents of Tacoma or immediate suburbs such as Fern Hill, Parkland, Spanaway, Ruston, or Regents Park—players in Puyallup, Sumner, and Roy are not eligible; (2) teams must deposit $5 before March 15 to be used for the purchase of stationary and baseballs; (3) an admission charge of 25¢ will be made at Athletic Park; (4) in the event of any person refusing to pay, the league president, the two managers, and the umpire will combine to eject him; (5) each team will be allowed 12 men and all players will be under contract; (6) morning games will start at 10:00 a.m., and there should be no complaint as during the summer months it is plenty warm enough at that time of the day.

Roy Wilkowski was the leading hitter in the City League in 1915 with a .459 batting average while playing for the Olympic Club entry. The team was runner-up to the champion South Tacoma Tigers, who added Wilkowski to the roster for the World Championship tournament in San Francisco.

The South Tacoma Tigers sailed to San Francisco aboard the *Admiral Schley* ship to play the White Autos team of Cleveland for the Amateur Baseball Championship of the World. The Tigers won the first game 3-2 behind southpaw hurler Orville Eley, but the Cleveland entry won the final two games 8-0 and 15-5 for the national amateur crown. Other team members included manager Walter Holmberg, Walt Hagedorn, Julian Shager, Roy Wilkowski, Oscar Jensen, Eddie McTighe, Paul Shager, Hank Crowl, Ob Woods, Ocky Haugland, Gus Davis, Nick Dahl, Les Patterson, and Jack Farrell.

The old "insane asylum" in Fort Steilacoom, Washington (now Lakewood), was renamed Western Washington Hospital for the Insane in 1886. This team played in the local league around 1910. The asylum was renamed Western State Hospital in 1915.

The Dupont baseball team of 1916 featured such notables as Jesse Baker (fourth from left), Roy Wilkowski (fourth from right), and Walt Hagedorn (far right). Baker pitched for the Chicago White Sox in 1911.

The Tacoma Foundation Company team played in the Shipyard League in 1918. Catcher Carl Stevens (top row, far left) was the hitting star of the club and was also the top hitter for the Tacoma Tigers entry in the Northwestern League that same season.

The Tacoma Elks were matched up against the Sound Tires on opening day played at Manitou Park on April 18, 1920. Sponsored by the Western Rubber Company, the Sound Tires nine was comprised of many players from the South Tacoma Tigers, including pitchers Walter "Ike" Isenberg and southpaw Les Harder. The Elks' entry had a strong team of ex-leaguers and semi-

pros, including pitcher Bert Hall and Earl Thompson, a top first baseman, but Isenberg and Harder each allowed only one hit as Sound Tires beat the Elks 1-0. (Washington State Historical Society, Tacoma, Boland Collection.)

OPPOSITE PAGE: The Sound Tire team played in the Valley League in 1920. Players are, from left to right, A.M. Elliott (factory manager), manager Bill Bither, Babe Helmecke, Oscar Jensen, Les Harder, George Anderson, Joe Hermsen, Tom Joues, James Chorlton, Walter Genin, Heinie Koessler, Walter Isenberg, Walter Holmberg, and George Hurtienne.

Teddy's Tigers, named after sponsor Teddy Christian who operated Teddy's Retreat, won the City League title in 1921 and 1922 against the K Street, Tacoma Avenue, Smelter AC, and Standard Oil teams. Team members include "Curley" Coen (1), George Johnson (2), Johnny Paddock (3), Vic Haugland (4), Cecil Erb (5), "Dad" Collier (6), Carlo Johnson (7), umpire Leo McQuarry (8), Ray Burkland (9), Frank Burkland (10), Fred Eldridge (11), Christian (12), Roy Wilkowski (13), Heinie Koessler (14), and Elmer Benson (15).

The Kay Street team poses prior to the opening game at Athletic Park in 1922. They went on to play in the state championship, losing 1-0 to Kelso. Team members are, from left to right, Bill Ryan, Oscar Jensen, Lou Balsano, Al Greco, Frank Balsano, Lee Keirstead, Joe Penowich, Joe Peterson, Sammy Cappa, Leo Kellogg, batboy Pat Jansen, Heinie Jansen, Rudy Becker, Oscar Larson, Cook Sypher, Ocky Haugland, Bill Weingarten, Art Berg, Charlie McLaughlin, Cliff Marker, and Mr. Taylor, a Kay Street merchant.

Shortstop Coley Anderson of the Twenty-third Street Skidoos finished the 1924 City League campaign with a .409 batting average to claim the hitting title. That was 11 points better than his nearest rival, outfielder Al Greco of the Kay Street club. Members of the Twenty-third Street club are, from left to right, (first row) Cliff Ellingson, Jake Otto, Archie Fife, unidentified, manager Shorty Couch, and Vic Haugland; (second row) Coley Anderson, Ski Wolner, Frank Hermsen, Al Amundson, Jim Kennedy, Lee Mowre, Bill Otto, and Art Swindland; the batboy is unidentified.

New York Yankee teammates Babe Ruth and Bob Meusel visited Tacoma on a barnstorming tour and played in an exhibition game at Stadium Bowl on October 18, 1924. Playing for the Tacoma City League All-Stars that included players representing K Street, Tacoma Avenue, Seventh Avenue, Fern Hill, and Twenty-third Street Skidoos, Ruth managed a double as his squad went on to defeat the Timber League All-Stars 5-3. From left to right are (first row) Allan Browne, Oscar Jensen, Ocky Haugland, Eddie Carlson, Johnny Paddock, Al Libke, Bane Browse, Coley Anderson, and *Tacoma Ledger* sports editor Dan Walton; (second row) Lee Keirstead, Johnny Larson, Bob Meusel, Babe Ruth, unidentified, batboy John Reha, Al Greco, and City League president Lorenzo Dow; (third row) Harley Franklin, Paul Wotten, unidentified, umpire Pomery, Lou Balsano, Bill Libke, Harold "Hick" Hayward (chairman of sponsorships for Edward B. Rhodes Post), umpire Clarence Stave, Shorty Couch, unidentified, and Sammy Cappa. (Washington State Historical Society, Tacoma, Boland Collection.)

Before the exhibition game, Babe Ruth and Bob Meusel got a shave at the Scobey Cigar Shop in downtown Tacoma, had breakfast at the Tacoma Hotel, greeted veterans at the Cushman Hospital, signed autographs at Rhodes Department Store, and visited with orphans at St. Ann's Home. Ruth (left) and Meusel (right) are shown here at the Cave, a confectionery located at 931 Broadway near the Pantages Theatre, where Miss Violet Slattery gave them chests of candy for their wives. (Karen Strand family.)

Dr. Williams B. Burns, a local dentist, poses with Babe Ruth at the Fircrest Golf Club on December 17, 1926. Ruth was in Tacoma to star in a vaudeville show at the Pantages Theatre. In his act, Ruth narrated silent films of his home-run heroics and demonstrated his swing, swatting a ball suspended by wire from the stage ceiling. The act concluded with the Babe inviting six youngsters onto the stage who were given autographed baseballs.

The City Lumber Company won the Commercial League in 1925, led by the .393 batting average of Holly Alshire and the pitching of Shorty Walgraf. The players from left to right are (first row) three unidentified and Shorty Walgraf; (second row) unidentified, Warren Alshire, Holly Alshire, and unidentified; (third row) two unidentified, Roy Harriman, Bill Libke, and Joe Earls. (Shanaman Sports Museum.)

The Kay Street nine, champions of the 1926 City League, met the Green Lake team from Seattle in a three-game series for the Kimball trophy at Athletic Park. The team was led by shortstop Al Pentecost (fifth from left), outfielder Al Greco (fourth from right), and slugging first baseman Lou Balsano (far right). Seven members of the Kay Street team hit over .300 for the season.

Lou Balsano was one of the most feared sluggers in the 1920s, and he powered the Kay Street club to City League titles in 1922 and 1926. Balsano also led the Timber League circuit in 1926 with a .405 batting average.

The Whistle Bottling Company, a bottler of carbonated beverages, was the forerunner of Cammarano Brothers. This photograph was taken in 1927 in front of the company's plant at 2314 Eighteenth A Street in Tacoma. From left to right are (first row) Rhine Thaut, Ted Lyphardt, Jack Otto, Fred Wilhelm, batboy Fred Noble, Ed Curran, and Joe Thiel; (second row) Howard Bailey, Bill Otto, Jack Zink, Ocky Larson, and unidentified; (third row) Bill Cammarano Sr., Dutch Thaut, unidentified, and Al Maruca.

A parade preceded opening day of the 1928 Tacoma City League season as the McKinley Hill Presidents team gathered around two new Chevys at Lincoln Bowl. With 2,000 fans in attendance, the 1927 champion Washington Co-ops defeated McKinley Hill 4-2, with Andy Anderson outdueling Ocky Haugland. (Tacoma Public Library.)

John Galbraith formed the Eatonville Lumber Company baseball team in the late 1920s. Galbraith was also the mayor of Eatonville from 1920 to 1941. Eatonville boasted a significant Japanese community from about 1900 to 1942, and this made up the majority of players on the team. They played other nearby town teams such as National, Tenino, and Rainier.

The Valley Forge team played in the Timber League in 1929 under manager A. C. "Butch" Sonntag (second row, far left). Team members included Wes Lees (first row, far right), Tony Banaszak Sr. (second row, far right) and Milt Woodard (second row, third from left). Woodard, a Stadium High and College of Puget Sound graduate, was president of the American Football League from 1966 to 1970 and helped merge the AFL with the NFL.

The Cammarano Brothers were longtime baseball team sponsors and on May 1, 1930, manager Al Greco (second row third from left) faced off against former teammate Sammy Cappa, manager of the Kay Street team, in a doubleheader at Lincoln Bowl. The Kay Streeters would shut out Cammarano 4-0. Players from left to right are (first row) John Chilia, two unidentified, Jack Otto, and Bill Otto; (second row) unidentified, Coley Anderson, Greco, Frank Balsano, unidentified, and Joe Thiel. (Tacoma Public Library, Boland Collection.)

The 1930 Valley League included the Eatonville Tigers, Rocky Ridge Ducks, Puyallup Berry Growers, Fife Cubs, South Prairie Wolves, Yelm Cougars, Orting Cardinals, and the Roy Wild Cats. In a pitching matchup between Fife's Fuzzy Elliott against Roy's Lefty Isekite, the Cubs broke through in the seventh inning to score three runs and win the pennant by a 3-2 score. From left to right are (first row) Murray, Bernie Myhre, Jim O'Ravez, Jake Otto, ? Phipps, and Bill Otto; (second row) ? Seigel, Roy Tarpening, ? Keys, manager Charley Hix, Herb Hall, Joe Kocha, and Lefty Isekite.

The Shaffer Box Company baseball team was crowned champions of the 1930 Industrial League. Notable players included Joe Salatino (back row, far left), Ernie Ruffo (back row, second from left), and Jim O'Ravez (front row, third from right). Salatino was a key member of the 1937 Johnson Paint team that placed fifth at the national tournament in Wichita, Kansas. Ruffo was the first Bellarmine athlete to earn four varsity letters in one year, and O'Ravez played at Camp Lewis for the Sixth Engineers club as well as Roy in the Valley League.

The 1934 Tacoma Tigers were a collection of players from the City League that formed a team to play in the Northwest Timber League. On June 28, the Tigers defeated the House of David nine, 6-4, behind the 15-strikeout, five-hit pitching of Vern Votaw. Handling the mound duties for the House of David team was Babe Didrikson, the famous all-around female athlete who gave up just one hit and three runs. From left to right are (first row) Wes Lees in suit, Hal Lennox, ? Hoefert, Joe Mlachnik, Cecil Erb, and Rudy Tollefson; (second row) Vern Votaw, Frank Ruffo, John Heinrick, Forrest Weingard, Joe Spadafore, and Vern Champagne.

Charlie Wry (pictured) pitched for the Gamble White Sox, and Vern Champagne, an outfielder for the Tacoma Tigers, was occasionally asked to fill in as a catcher for the team. On those occasions, umpire Clarence Stave, in his most eloquent manner, would announce the battery for the day as "Wry and Champagne." According to Champagne, "The crowd thought we were the bartenders!"

Frank Ruffo played for Cammarano Brothers and the Johnson Paint team in the City League and the Tacoma Tigers in the Timber League. The slugger was awarded a coupon good for one free T-bone steak from the Mecca Restaurant when he hit a home run off of Hall of Fame pitcher Grover Cleveland Alexander, who was in town on a barnstorming tour. Earlier in the season, Frank won a coupon from the Red Rooster Barber Shop good for a free haircut, shave, and shampoo for hitting the first round-tripper of the season.

The Tacoma Electrochemical Company team won consecutive Commercial League titles in 1934 and 1935. It was commonplace for players to compete on two or three teams each week, which explains the different uniforms being worn. The company later became a part of Pennsylvania Salt Manufacturing Company of Washington. (Tacoma Public Library.)

Superior Dairy won the 1935 City League with three players who would go on to play for the Tacoma Tigers of the Western International League—Cy Greenlaw, Les Bishop, and John Milroy. The team also featured College of Puget Sound standout Jimmy Ennis and the Haugland brothers, Ocky and Vic. From left to right are (first row) manager Ocky Haugland, Rick Johnson, Ken Doxon, Joey Peterson, Mike Pavolka, Ennis, Milroy, and Harry Eagles; (second row) Otto Smith, Joe Thiel, Vic Haugland, Carl Schildt, Bill Gourley, Cy Greenlaw, Art Berg, Joe Bowers, and Les Bishop; the mascot is "Tubby" Stark.

The bleachers at Lincoln High School were filled to capacity with fans watching the first game of the 1935 Tacoma City League season between Superior Dairy and the Beacon Oilers. Joe Bowers singled to right field, just past a diving Doug Hendry as Les Bishop scored from third. Coaching the bases for the Dairymen were Ocky Haugland (third base) and Joey Peterson (first base). Watching the play were catcher Al Libke, pitcher Ed Colbo, first baseman Bud Bittner, and legendary umpire Clarence Stave. (Tacoma Public Library.)

The 1937 Johnson Paint team, managed by John Heinrick, was the first team from Tacoma to travel beyond the West Coast to participate in a national tournament. In Wichita, Kansas, to compete in the National Baseball Congress tournament, the team went 3-2 and finished fifth. To raise funds for the trip, the team played an exhibition game in front of 3,500 fans in Lincoln Bowl who watched Freddie Steele, world middleweight boxing champion, play three innings in right field for the Painters. From left to right are (first row) Frank Ruffo, Jim Ennis, batboy Sam Baker, Rudy Tollefson, Doug Hendry, and Joe Mlachnick: (second row) Hal Lee, Rick Lewis, John Heinrick, Andy Padovan, Morry Abbott, Erling Tollefson, and an unidentified boy; (third row) Fred Hutchinson, Earl Johnson, Joe Dailey, Cy Greenlaw, Joe Salatino, Loris Baker, and Dutch Scheffler.

The Casino Tavern team of 1941 featured Jimmy Claxton (second row, fourth from left) and Jess Brooks (first row, second from left). Claxton, who pitched for the Oakland Oaks of the Pacific Coast League on May 28,1916, just happened to be on the roster when a candy company's photographer was in town to take photographs for Zeenuts baseball cards. Even though Claxton was released a week later, he was around long enough to have his own baseball card. It is now valued at over $2,000 because he was the first African American to ever be depicted on a baseball card. The "Casinos" played in the Western Washington League and included the Tillicum Chiefs, Spanaway, the Morton Loggers, Pacific City, Roy, and the Shipbuilders. Owned by Alfonso Harden, the Casino Tavern was located at 1328 Broadway Street.

In August 1942, the Tillicum Chiefs of Western State Hospital, who played in the Twilight League, had won 23 games and were in the playoffs for the circuit title. From left to right are (first row) Bus Mitchell, Lornie Merkle, Johnny Ward, Dewey West, and Bob Huegel; (second row) manager Clink Jacobs, Dick Smith, Fred Hebert, unidentified patient who served as mascot, Howard Johnson, Phil Jacobs, and business manager Garry Robinson.

As the 1940s progressed, thoughts of RBIs and road trips were replaced by the concern with the war around the world. City league teams had a difficult time maintaining full rosters, so the Shipbuilders Athletic Club put together a Tacoma team that had outstanding players from past years, as well as some younger men. Among those shown in this 1942 photograph are, from left to right, (first row) Gene Hansen (first) and Dave Goodman (eighth); (second row) Mayor Harry Cain (fourth), Harry Hall (seventh), Bob Garretson (eleventh), and Roy Johnson (thirteenth). Roy Johnson enjoyed a major-league career like his younger brother Bob, playing from 1929 to 1938 in the outfield for the Detroit Tigers, Boston Red Sox, and New York Yankees.

The Kay Street club won the 1949 City League Championship, edging McKinley Avenue and Thirty-eighth Street for top honors. Other teams in the circuit included Sixth Avenue, Twenty-sixth and Proctor Streets, and South Tacoma. The Kay Street entry was led by pitchers Art Viafore and Pete Sabutis; infielders Cliff Schiesz, Earl Birnel, Dave Minnitti, and Frank Morrone; outfielders Pete Mello and Frank Bonaro; and catcher Hal Schimling.

Managed by veteran catcher Hal Schimling, the Olde Pilsner team played in the 1951 Sunset League won by Busch's Drive-In under the leadership of Doug McArthur and Vern Kohout. From left to right are (first row) Doc ?, Hal Schimling, Eddie Wheeler, an unidentified batboy, Bob Jamison, Cliff Schiesz, and Frank Karwoski; (second row) Dale Bloom, Fred Rickert, Tom Absher, Ron Billings, Bob Johnson, Hank Semmern, Jim Stanton, and Gerry Hefty.

The Tacoma Athletics played an independent schedule in 1951 against town teams such as Buckley and Enumclaw. Four members played at one time for the Tacoma Tigers of the Western International League, including Marv Rickert, Fred Rickert, Pete Sabutis, and Bill Funk. Pictured from left to right are (first row) Joe Stortini, Jack Murphy, Marv Rickert, Dick Schlosstein, Pete Sabutis, and Gordy Hersey; (second row) Don Rasmussen, Funk, unidentified, Fred Rickert, Hank Semmern, and two unidentified.

When the South End Boys Club opened in 1954, Tom Cross contacted Don Danielson (second row, far right) about a program started by inmates at McNeil Island who would use their own resources to purchase baseball uniforms and equipment for local youth teams. The inmates had a contest to name the team and chose the Little Giants. The prison population was kept informed about the games, and at the end of the season the team was invited to the island with another local team where they played before a large, "captive" audience. The inmates were so taken up with the program that the sponsorship was expanded to include basketball and football.

The 1955 Spanaway baseball team won the Valley League's southern division and met northern division champion Western State Hospital at Cheney Field in Tacoma for the league crown. From left to right are (first row) batboy Gary Justice, Gene Reardon, Jim Leap, Howard Davis, Jim Rediske, and Dick Hansch; (second row) Frank Failey, Art Thiel, Ted Harris, Ray Brammer, Bob Kuper, and Buzz Eley.

Sponsored by Stan Naccarato and Morley Brotman, the Stanley Shoemen won the Amateur Baseball Congress's national championship in 1956 behind pitchers Dale Bloom and Mike Dillon, catcher Jack Johnson, and outfielders Bob Maguinez and Earl Hyder. From left to right are (first row) Ron Storaasli, Pat Dillon, George Grant, Manly Mitchell, Doug McArthur, Hyder, Jim Harney, Maguinez, and Dick Montgomery; (second row) Gordy Grubert, Johnson, Dick Schlosstein, Monte Geiger, Bloom, Jim Gallwas, Dillon, Max Braman, and scorekeeper Tom Montgomery.

Team sponsor Stan Naccarato presents a bouquet of roses to Arlene McArthur, wife of manager Doug McArthur of the national champion Stanley Shoemen team, upon their return home from Battle Creek, Michigan.

Doug McArthur (left) has two national championships on his resume: one as coach of the 1956 Stanley Shoemen team and the other as athletic director at the University of Puget Sound when the Loggers won the NCAA Division II basketball crown in 1976. Besides coaching Busch's Drive-in in the Sunset and Valley Leagues, McArthur also coached the Cheney Studs for a season. He is shown here with umpires Frank Morrone and Lornie Merkle (right). (Shanaman Sports Museum.)

In 1956, Dave Harkness Sr. had the privilege of coaching his five sons on the Boilermakers Local 568–sponsored team that played for Roy in the Valley League. From left to right they are (first row) Gene, Gary, and Dave Jr.; (second row) Val, Dave Sr., and Ray.

Morley Brotman (center) presents the 1957 Washington State Baseball Association's state championship trophy to sponsor Alden Woodworth (left) as manager Marv Scott looks on. The club missed out on qualifying for the national championship that year but finished runner-up in 1958. Key players included pitchers Rod Keough and Bill Funk, infielder George Grant, and catcher Arley Kangas, a member of the USA Pan-American team in 1959 and the only Tacoman to ever be selected.

Bob Maguinez started playing baseball in the City League in 1947 at the age of 16 and was an All-Tournament selection for the Shoemen's national championship team. Known as "Mac" to everyone, he played for the Woodworth nine when they took second and was on the Cheney Studs' national title team in 1960. Bob umpired for 18 years and scouted for the Yankees and Twins' organizations.

Earl Hyder (batting) played amateur baseball in the area's City, Sunset, and Valley Leagues for more than a dozen years with unparalleled success. Earl played center field on the 1956 Stanley Shoemen club and then helped the Woodworth Contractors to a second-place finish in 1958. Hyder saved the best for last, as his two-run homer in 1960 against Detroit in the title game helped the Cheney Studs take home the trophy. His .550 average earned him All-America honors.

Throughout the 1950s, old-timers' all-star teams traveled to McNeil Island to put on exhibition games for the inmates. Most of the players were in their 40s and 50s, but they were still talented and their passion for the sport was unsurpassed. From left to right are (first row) Frank "Bush" Tobin, Al Pentecost, Pete Mello, Joe Mlachnik, Walt Jutte, Bob Johnson, Sonny Bailey, and Dick Greco; (second row) Cy Rubado, Jeff Heath, Hank Semmern, Bill Libke, Chet Johnson, Art Berg, Marv Rickert, Les Bishop, Vern Morris, and Del Michalson.

The Tacoma-Pierce County community has had its share of homegrown athletes who parlayed their start on the sandlots into highly successful major-league careers. Bob Johnson played for the Philadelphia Athletics for 10 of his 13 seasons in the major leagues and compiled a lifetime batting average of .296, hit 288 career home runs, and was also chosen to the American League All-Star squad seven times. He was the fifth player to have nine consecutive seasons of 20 or more home runs, he batted .300 five times, had eight seasons with 100 runs batted in, and finished with 1,283 RBIs.

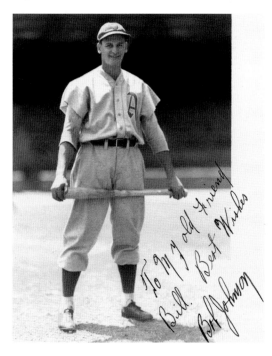

CAP PETERSON   CLEVELAND INDIANS

Cap Peterson was a 1962 graduate of Clover Park high and played for the Tacoma Giants in 1963 and the Tacoma Twins in 1972. Cap played five seasons with the San Francisco Giants, two with the Washington Senators, and one with the Cleveland Indians.

Uncle Sam had a say in the career paths for, from left to right, (first row) Steve Whitaker and Ron Cey and (second row) Rick Austin and Bill Murphy, but the Army was kind enough to station all four at Ft. Lewis, where they found time to keep their arms in shape and hitting skills sharp. Austin, a 1965 Lakes High grad, played two years with both the Indians and Milwaukee and one season in Japan. Austin's overall major-league record was 4-8 with a 4.63 ERA. Murphy, a Clover Park High grad, made his major-league debut with the New York Mets in 1966 as a center fielder.

Steve Whitaker, a 1962 Lincoln High grad, debuted with the New York Yankees in 1966 and proceeded to hit seven home runs in his first 16 days, including a grand slam and an inside-the-park home run in a three-day span. In 1967, he batted in front of Mickey Mantle and Roger Maris while hitting .243 with 11 home runs and 50 RBIs. He played for the Seattle Pilots in 1969 and finished with the San Francisco Giants in 1970.

Ron Cey, a 1966 Mt. Tahoma High grad, spent 11 seasons with the Los Angeles Dodgers, starting in 1971. He played in four World Series, winning it all in 1981 along with being named co-MVP. Cey was named to six straight all-star games (74-79), as well as hitting the fifth-most home runs in Dodgers history. Known as the "Penguin," he played five more seasons with the Cubs (1983–1986) and the A's (1987). Cey finished his career with 316 home runs.

Doug Sisk, a Stadium High grad, played for the New York Mets from 1982 through the 1987 season and was a member of the 1986 Mets team that beat the Boston Red Sox in the World Series. As an all-star game alternate in 1984, Doug notched a career-best 15 saves and a 2.09 earned run average. He also played for the Baltimore Orioles and Atlanta Braves and ended his career with a 22-20 record, 33 saves, and a 3.27 earned run average.

A Bellarmine Prep grad, Jon Lester was named the Gatorade State Player of the Year for Washington in 2000. Lester made his major-league debut against the Texas Rangers on June 10, 2006, and in the 2007 World Series he won the series-clinching game pitching almost six shutout innings. He was a 19-game winner in 2010 for the Red Sox and was a candidate for the Cy Young award.

PROFESSIONAL BASEBALL
1890–1922

Professional baseball reached the Pacific Northwest in 1890, when Tacoma joined Seattle, Portland, and Spokane Falls for the inaugural season of the Pacific Northwest League. In the early years, future Hall of Famers Clark Griffith, Walter Johnson, and Iron Joe McGinnity wore Tacoma uniforms.

Tacoma's first home grounds were established at Eleventh and L Streets, formally named Tacoma Baseball Park, in the neighborhood known as Hilltop. General admission was 50¢ and the grandstand was 75¢. Seattle won the season opener 7-6.

In an effort to increase excitement in the preseason, the Ledger newspaper predicted, "The Tacoma team of 1891, from all indications, will be a daisy." Unfortunately the Daisies finished last. The Daisies of 1892 were much better, and included Griffith, a right-handed pitcher who was a veteran of five professional seasons at the age of 22.

Financial uncertainties kept league alignments to a minimum for the next several years until John McCloskey helped resurrect the PNL in 1901 and adopted the Tigers as their nickname.

Following transfer of the Sacramento team to Tacoma, the Tigers won their first Pacific Coast League crown in 1904. It was a short stay, however, as the small paying crowds made it financially unfeasible to continue, so the club was transferred back to Sacramento for the balance of 1904 and then relocated to Fresno for the start of the 1906 season.

In 1905, the Tigers played in the Northwestern League under principal stockholder, George Shreeder, who hired Mike Lynch as player/manager. Lynch quickly became the city's first long-term professional baseball figure.

The Tigers moved into a new ballpark in 1907 at Fourteenth and Sprague Streets, called Athletic Park, and enjoyed several good seasons. Unfortunately a last-place finish in 1912 cost Lynch his job and Shreeder a lot of money, opening the door for former major-league star Joe McGinnity to become part-owner and manager.

With the start of World War I in 1917, the military draft took players away from teams that were already suffering from low gate receipts, and the league suspended operations in mid-July. A new Pacific Coast International League was subsequently formed, but it was not until 1920 that it actually completed an entire season, with the Tacoma entry finishing fourth.

Another reorganization preceded the 1922 season, with Tacoma and Vancouver joining Calgary and Edmonton in a four-team circuit dubbed the Western International League, but it only lasted one year.

Other than Pacific Coast League games at Seattle and Portland, Northwest fans saw no more pro ball until Tacoma and five other cities formed a new Western International League as the Depression began to wind down in 1937.

Tacoma, Seattle, Spokane, and Portland formed the Pacific Northwest League, and professional baseball made its debut on May 3, 1890, when the Tacoma entry dropped a 7-6 decision to the Seattle nine. It was not until 1901 that the Pacific Northwest League was reborn with John McCloskey as the manager of the newly nicknamed Tacoma Tigers. Tacoma finished second behind Portland in league play but boasted the circuit's leading hitter in Charley McIntrye, who hit .341 and was the top fielding third baseman as well. Teammate Jimmy St. Vrain, a left-handed pitcher, won 27 games.

PROFESSIONAL BASEBALL: 1890–1922

By the time the 1902 season rolled around, the league membership had increased to six teams with the addition of teams in Butte and Helena. Infielder Jay Andrews managed Tacoma. With only one returning player, Andrews, who took his place at third, probably was his own best player. Butte won the championship that year, while the Tigers failed to contend and finished fifth, winning 48 games and losing 72. (David Eskenazi collection.)

By February of 1904, the Pacific Coast League was up and running with the Sacramento franchise being transferred to Tacoma. The team performed at the Eleventh Street Grounds with admission just 25¢ and Col. Mike Fisher managing the Tigers. Bobby Keefe, who won 34 games, was the staff star, but Orval "Giant" Overall burst onto the scene and won 32 games and lost 25. Tacoma added Jimmy St. Vrain, Lou Nordyke, and Mike Lynch, a standout with the local Pacific National League club, to nine holdovers from Sacramento's second-place team, and the resulting aggregation brought the city its first pro championship by finishing first in both halves of a 224-game split season. From left to right are (first row) Jack Fitzgerald, St. Vrain, Tom Sheehan, and Happy Hogan; (second row) Bill Thomas, Overall, Charley Graham, manager Fisher, Nordyke, Lynch, and Charles Doyle; (third row) Perle Casey, Truck Eagan, Dave Evans, Dean Worley, George Shreeder, Keefe, and George McLaughlin.

PROFESSIONAL BASEBALL: 1890–1922

In 1906, George Shreeder, owner of a popular saloon called the Olympic Club, acquired the Everett franchise, moved it to Tacoma, and convinced Mike Lynch to stay in town as the player/manager for the Tigers. Led by Lynch, who won the batting title with a .355 mark, Tacoma won the Northwestern League pennant. On April 30, Lynch auditioned an 18-year-old pitcher from Southern California named Walter Johnson. After Grays Harbor beat the young right-hander 4-3, Lynch, who never lived it down, sent him home. Johnson pitched for a semi-pro team in Weiser, Idaho, before joining the Washington Senators, winning 416 games, and becoming an original member of the Baseball Hall of Fame.

Pitcher Ike Butler (second row, far right) was the bright spot for the Tigers with his 32 victories in 1907, and he followed that up with another 19 during the 1908 season. The Tigers, who played 13 more games than Aberdeen, lost eight of them and finished second in 1907 behind the Black Cats, who won the league title based on a higher wining percentage. (David Eskenazi collection.)

With the success of his 1906 club, George Shreeder had a new ballpark—Athletic Park—at Fourteenth and Sprague Streets constructed and ready to go for the 1907 season. The Tigers finished in second place with a 90-59 record that year. Tacoma manager Mike Lynch (standing, far right) coaches third base while Spokane's defense includes catcher Charlie Swindells, pitcher Ervin Jensen, first baseman Dave Rowan, third sacker Joe Altman, and umpire Piggy Ward calling balls and strikes. (David Eskenazi collection.)

It was another runner-up finish for the Tigers in 1908 under Mike Lynch who, at age 32, hit .253—30 percentage points behind team leader Doc Suess. The season also saw the debut of Bert Hall, an 18-year-old pitcher who played for the Tigers for the next five seasons, compiling a 53-54 record. September 27, 1908, was a notable day, as Tacoma beat visiting Spokane three times in the only tripleheader in Northwest baseball history, defeating the Indians 4-1 in a morning contest and then 7-0 and 7-3 in an afternoon doubleheader.

Following the 1908 season, Mike Lynch left to
manage Seattle, which opened the door for Russ Hall
to become business manager of the Tigers for the
next two seasons, while catcher Cliff Blankenship
and pitcher Ike Butler handled the managerial duties.
But, with a team batting average of just .212, the
Tigers ended the season with a 64-111 record. Hall
(center), holding a "buck" in one hand, a beer in the
other, and one of his favorite "cobs" in his mouth,
looks on as Eddie Miller makes an "Angleworm
Cocktail." Looking on is Leo Kellogg, proprietor of
the Kellogg Pool Hall and lunch counter at Eleventh
and K Streets, who later managed the Kay Street
baseball club.

P.C. LEAGUE
SEASON 1913
BAKER
SAN FRAN.

One of the few bright spots for the Tigers in 1909
occurred early in the season when the Tigers defeated
Vancouver, 1-0, on a three-hitter by southpaw Jesse
Baker. Baker, who had been born in a log cabin on
Anderson Island, lost 23 games for Tacoma before
being traded to Spokane but still led the league with
249 strikeouts. He became the first player from Pierce
County to play in the major leagues when he donned
a Chicago White Sox uniform in 1911 and fashioned
a 2-7 record. He played for the San Francisco Seals of
the Pacific Coast League in 1912 and 1913.

Eddie Quinn (left), new owner of the Tacoma Tigers in 1910, was a believer in advertising and sent manager Cliff Blankenship (right) to a sporting-goods firm to place an order for patches to be reproduced with a depiction of the "great mountain" and the words "Mt. Tacoma" inscribed below with the plan to stitch them on the back of their road uniforms and on their sweaters. Tacoma finished third in the four-team Northwestern League race. (David Eskenazi collection.)

Anson Mott was one of the league's top fielding first basemen during the 1910 season. (David Eskenazi collection.)

Mike Lynch's Tacoma Tigers opened their 1911 season against the Victoria Bees at Athletic Park in Tacoma. Before a crowded estimated at more than 3,000, Victoria's two pitchers combined to throw a no-hitter for a 3-0 victory. A parade of 19 autos and a marching band along Pacific and Broadway Streets preceded the game. Mike Lynch (standing against car) and Victoria manager Eddie Householder rode in the first car. Occupying a prominent spot with the team was the Tigers' new mascot, Tige—a little bantam rooster brought up from Southern California. (David Eskenazi collection.)

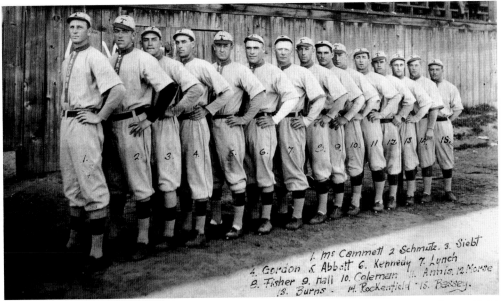

The 1911 Tacoma Tigers ball club finished fifth in the Northwestern League with an 81-84 record under manager Mike Lynch. Most of these players were available on Obak cigarette baseball cards that were produced during the season; the cards were found inside the cigarette packs themselves. (David Eskenazi collection.)

Pitcher Blaine Gordon had a 16-14 record for the Tacoma Tigers in 1911. (David Eskenazi collection.)

Second baseman Curt Coleman played in 452 games for Tacoma from 1909 to 1911, and during his three seasons for the Tigers he hit .228, .219, and .268, respectively. Coleman made his major-league debut in 1912 with the New York Highlanders. (David Eskenazi collection.)

A last-place finish in 1912 sent manager Mike Lynch packing and presented former New York Giants' star, Joe McGinnity, with the opportunity to become part-owner and player/manager the following year. From left to right are (first row) Rabbit Nill, Bill Yohe, Cy Neighbors, Richard Crittenden, Elmer Crieger, unidentified, and Ike Butler; (second row) Don Cameron, Charlie Schmutz, Bill Ludwig, Eddie Higgins, Con Starkel, David Goodman, Mike Lynch, Blain Gordon, unidentified, Ody Abbott, and unidentified.

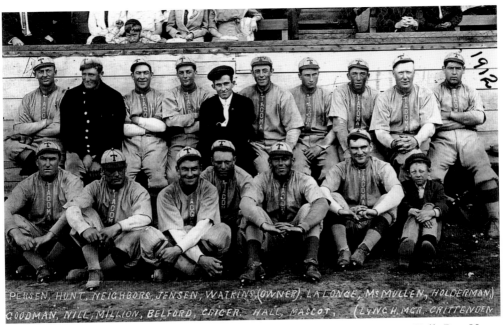

Despite a dismal showing in the 1912 league standings, Ody Abbott, Bert Hall, Ben Hunt, Bill Ludwig, Mike Lynch, Fred McMullin, Hap Morse, Cy Neighbors, Rabbit Nill, Charlie Schmutz, and Bill Yohe all got a taste of the major leagues before their careers ended. (David Eskenazi collection.)

Edd Watkins (left) owned the Tacoma Tigers in 1912 before Joe McGinnity took over ownership in 1913. McGinnity and Frank Redpath purchased the ball club and Athletic Park for $20,000 and then invested additional funds to upgrade the venue to seat 6,000 fans, including 200 box seats. McGinnity, Walter Johnson, and Clark Griffith, who helped Tacoma finish second in the Pacific Northwest League in 1892, all were pitchers with a Tacoma connection now enshrined in the Baseball Hall of Fame.

At age 42, rather than telling his players what to do, player/manager Joe McGinnity showed them, appearing in a league-high 68 games in 1913 while compiling a 22-19 record in an incredible 436 innings, which also led the Northwestern League.

Ten Million (left), who played under Joe McGinnity in 1913 and 1914, graduated from Seattle's Broadway High School in 1908. A prominent Seattle judge, Ten got his name because, with the last name of Million, his mother wanted her son to stand out. When the daughter of Ten and his wife, Christine, was born, his grandmother bribed them with $50 to name her Decillian Million for the same reason. Later Decillian used the name Dixie, but in her early years she was known as Decillian Million, daughter of Ten Million.

After managing 75 wins the previous season, Tacoma slipped back to 64 victories in 1914 with Joe McGinnity earning 20 of them. Local product Cy Neighbors led the club with a .315 batting average, while third baseman Fred McMullin (first row, third from right) was second on the team at .293. McMullin later became one of eight Chicago White Sox players banned as part of the 1919 World Series scandal.

Fremont "Goo" Campbell Jr., who owned shares in the Tacoma baseball club, played on various Northwest League teams in the areas including the Amocats. He served as Pierce County sheriff from 1931 to 1935. (David Eskenazi collection.)

The Tigers captured second place in the Northwestern League in 1915 with an 85-73 record, just behind the Seattle entry. Outfielder Les Wilson led the loop with 54 steals, and Edson Johnson displayed his patience at the plate with a league-leading 74 walks. In three seasons, Joe McGinnity (third row, second from the right) compiled a 63-55 record as a pitcher, including a 21-15 record in 1915 in his last season at the age of 44.

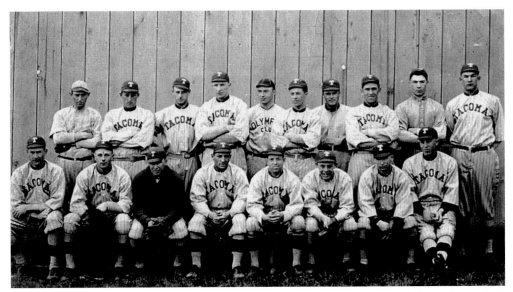

Due to the war, the Northwestern League shut down in mid-July of 1917 with Frank "Tealey" Raymond (first row, second from right) at the helm. Harry Harper won the batting crown with a .382 average, while 20 year-old Herm Pillette (second row, far right) made his professional debut with the Tigers. Pillette would go on to enjoy a career that spanned 26 years.

When Tacoma took the field in 1918 it was under the banner of the Pacific Coast International League, but the war in Europe was hurting baseball attendance. The Tigers and Spokane did not even make it through the first month, dropping out of the league in late May. The Tigers are shown here playing in Vancouver, British Columbia. (David Eskenazi collection.)

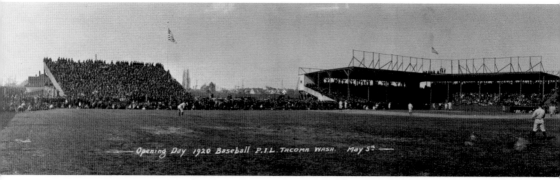

Opening Day 1920 Baseball P.I.L. Tacoma Wash. May 5th

On May 5, 1920, Tacoma's baseball lovers broke all previous opening-day records when 9,328 fans watched the Tigers beat the Islanders 5-1 in the debut game of the Pacific Coast International League under the leadership of President Louis H. Burnett of Tacoma. The game was preceded by a parade of over 500 cars and decorated floats that ended at Athletic Park. Under the leadership of Burnett, the league played at a Class B level and consisted of the Seattle Giants, Spokane

Indians, Vancouver Beavers, Yakima Indians, Victoria, and Tacoma. Victoria won the league crown despite Tacoma finishing second in batting and fielding among the six teams. Bert Cole was the top pitcher in the league, compiling a 24-7 win-loss record with 29 complete games and 166 strikeouts. (Washington State Historical Society, Tacoma.)

Carl Stevens was a fixture on the diamond in Tacoma with the Tigers for five seasons, starting in 1915. Stevens had seven hits in a 31-12 outburst against Butte in 1917 and was the leading hitter for Tacoma in 1918 with a .368 average before the club folded after just 19 games. A catcher, Stevens hit .307 in 1920 and .315 in 1921.

THE WESTERN INTERNATIONAL LEAGUE 1937–1951

The last professional league that Tacoma competed in during the early years was the Western International League (WIL) in 1922, where they finished fourth behind Calgary, Edmonton, and Vancouver. It would be another 15 years before pro ball returned to Tacoma, when the Tigers, Lewiston (Idaho), Spokane, Vancouver (Canada), Wenatchee, and Yakima formed a new WIL.

Roger W. Peck, a Tacoma banker, was elected president of the new Class B circuit. Games were played at Athletic Park, complete with a rebuilt grandstand. League play started on April 27, 1937, and while Wenatchee won the first half, the Tigers bounced back to win the second half and then trounced the Chiefs fours games to one in the postseason playoffs. Lefty Isekite and Alden Wilkie led the Tigers in pitching and Harvey Storey led the offense with a .347 average.

It was a roller coaster ride for the Tigers as they finished last in 1938 only to turn around in 1939 and clobber 108 round-trippers compared to only 31 the previous season. Tacoma native Morry Abbott, who belted 37 home runs, led Tacoma, and the club had another championship to boast about.

Despite a fourth-place finish in 1940, the Tigers rose to the challenge in the playoffs, winning their third WIL crown in four seasons. Following the 1942 season, the Western International League did not operate for the remainder of the war.

Tacoma's 1946 club played on new grounds in Tiger Park, located at Thirty-eighth and Lawrence Streets. The Tigers finished fourth with three local products leading the way—catcher Earl Kuper, pitcher Cy Greenlaw, and 21 year-old Dick Greco, who clouted 15 dingers in his pro rookie season.

In 1947, Kuper won the batting championship with a record .389 mark, and in 1948 Greco elevated his game a notch, batting .346 and driving in 126 runs.

The Tigers skidded downward again in 1949, winding up seventh, under former American League slugger "Indian" Bob Johnson. Greco led the league with 33 home runs while driving in 118 runs and scoring 123. .

In 1950, the parent Padres assigned Jim Brillheart to manage the Tigers, who improved dramatically by winning 90 games and losing 58 to finish only one game behind Yakima's repeat champion. The 1951 team, however, lacked punch as well as pitching depth, and their sixth-place showing was predictable. Beset with financial problems, the Padres called it quits and sold the franchise to a group of Lewiston, Idaho, businessmen.

In their first year of the Class B Western International League, the Tigers defeated the Wenatchee Chiefs four games to one to win the WIL crown. They were led by third sacker Harvey Storey's 18 round-trippers and a .347 batting average for the season and the pitching of Aldon Wilkie and Floyd "Lefty" Isekite.

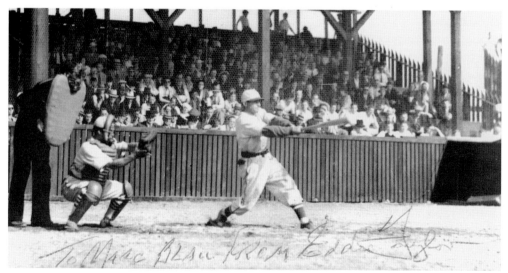

Eddie Taylor, second baseman and manager of the 1937 Tacoma Tigers, connected for a double in his first at-bat against the Vancouver Maple Leafs in the second game of a double header on May 2, 1937. Athletic Park, located at 1302 South Sprague Avenue, was filled with a capacity crowd. The Tigers won the first game 3-1 but lost the second 10-5. (Tacoma Public Library, Richards Collection.)

In 1937, Jerry Geehan joined KMO Radio and became the first play-by-play broadcaster for the Tacoma Tigers of the Western International League. He was owner and general manager of KTAC Radio from 1952 to 1969, the station that broadcasted Tacoma Giants and Cubs games.

Floyd "Lefty" Isekite of the Tacoma Tigers had a blazing fastball and tossed a no-hitter in 1937 against the Wenatchee Chiefs. Lefty amassed a four-year career record of 61-40 with 819 strikeouts, leading the league in the latter category three consecutive seasons (1938 to 1940). (Tacoma Public Library, Richards Collection.)

One of the most talked about players when the Western International League opened was Ernie Raimondi, Tacoma's 17-year-old third sacker. Ernie hit .299 in his first year with the Tigers and showed flashes of brilliance as he hit .337 in his second season with the club before moving on to play for the San Francisco Seals. Raimondi's promising career was cut short when he was killed in France during the war in 1945.

A record capacity crowd of 6,000 fans crammed into the bleachers, spilling out onto the infield to witness the May 5, 1938, hometown debut of the Tacoma Tigers at Athletic Park. Despite all of the enthusiasm, the defending champion Tigers lost to Yakima 8-7. (Tacoma Public Library, Richards Collection.)

THE WESTERN INTERNATIONAL LEAGUE: 1937–1951

The 1938 Tacoma Tigers finished last in the six-team Western International League but did produce a batting champion in Dave Goodman (first row, fourth from left), who hit .337 for the season. The team featured Tacoma's Les Bishop (first row, third from right) and Floyd Isekite (second row, fourth from left), along with Longbranch's Marv Rickert (second row, fourth from right). Rickert played six years in the major leagues and appeared in the 1948 World Series with the Boston Braves.

Larry Powell was a standout southpaw hurler for Tacoma in 1938, finishing with a 14-10 record and 230 strikeouts, 18 less than teammate and league strikeout leader, Lefty Isekite.

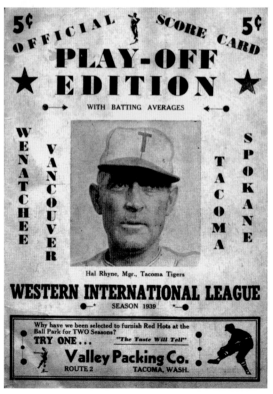

Hal Rhyne, Mgr., Tacoma Tigers

The 1939 Tacoma Tigers defeated Spokane three games to one and then knocked off the Wenatchee Chiefs four games to two to win their second "Willy League" championship. From left to right are (sitting) Gene Kelly; (first row) manager Hal Rhyne, Neil Clifford, Bob Garretson, Morry Abbott, Jack Colbern, and Vince Harriman; (second row) Walt Mattos, Carl Brady, Herm Reich, Al Miller, Gordon Mann, Ray Medeghini, Bob Cole, Floyd Isekite, and Ralph Mountain.

Hal Rhyne skippered the Tacoma Tigers to the Western International League title in 1939 and then shared managerial duties with first baseman Bob Garretson as the club won a second consecutive title in 1940.

From left to right are Herm Reich, Bob Garretson, Ralph Mountain, and Morry Abbott, who provided most of the run production in 1939. Reich hit .299 and was second on the team with 91 RBIs, while Garretson was the second-leading hitter for the Tigers with a .315 average and leading the team in hits with 167. Mountain hit a solid .274, and Tacoman Morry Abbott clouted 37 home runs and had 123 RBIs to lead the way in his first season with the club.

These players are, from left to right, catcher Neil Clifford, center fielder Herm Reich, and first baseman Bob Garretson. They are joining manager Hal Rhyne in a visit to Tacoma General Hospital on June 9, 1939.

Charley Schanz was the ace of the 1942 Tacoma Tigers staff, finishing the season with an 18-13 record and a 3.00 ERA. Schanz pitched in the major leagues for the Philadelphia Phillies for four seasons and later on was a member of the Seattle Rainiers' 1951 Pacific Coast League championship team.

Tiger Park, as viewed in 1946 on opening day, was located at South Thirty-eighth and Lawrence Streets and was a trifle larger than Sick's Stadium in Seattle, home of the Rainiers. Right field down the foul line was 330 feet away, while the left-field foul pole was 352 feet away. The power alleys in right center and left center were 390 feet and 395 feet, respectively, and dead center was 410 feet compared to 405 feet at Sick's.

The 1946 Tigers finished fourth with a 76-67 record. Local area players on the club included Earl Kuper, Dick Greco, Cy Greenlaw, Marv Scott, Morry Abbott, Fred Rickert, Gene Hansen, and Marion Oppelt and outfielder Henry Vallee, who went on to become construction foreman when Cheney Stadium was built in 1960.

Tacoma hosted a Jubilee Parade on June 25, 1946, ostensibly to celebrate the fact that World War II was over. A sense of history and pride led the South Tacoma community to sponsor the Tacoma Tigers' float, shown passing the corner of South Tenth Street and Pacific Avenue.

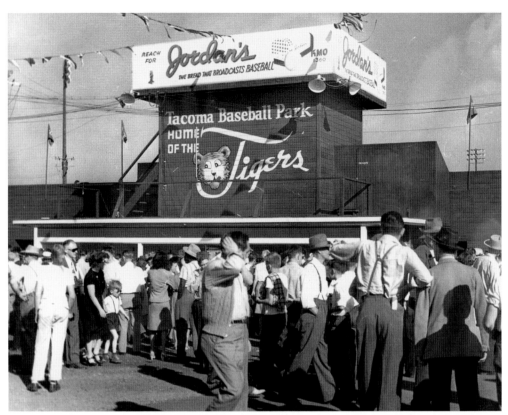

Clay Huntington and Rod Belcher began broadcasting Tacoma Tigers games on KMO 1360 in 1946. Clay got his start by practicing play-by-play while perched in a tree overlooking the neighborhood vacant lot while his friends played ball. During his years with the Tigers, he was appropriately referred to as Jordan's Breadcaster, as the broadcasts were sponsored by Jordan's Bread Company.

Thanks in large part to World War II, Cy Greenlaw never made it to the major leagues—or the Pacific Coast League for that matter—but the rangy left-handed pitcher from Kapowsin occupies a special place in local baseball lore. Cy joined the Tacoma Tigers of the Class B Western International League and was an 18-game winner in 1946, pitching a 3-0, seven-inning no-hitter against the Yakima Stars at Tiger Park. In fact, Greenlaw is one of only 14 pitchers to ever throw a no-hitter in local professional baseball history.

The Tacoma Tigers were sold to the San Diego Padres Baseball Club of the Pacific Coast League for $109,000 in October 1947. The sale included the Tacoma Tigers Park property, the players, team franchise in the Western International League, and all other franchises and privileges of the club. (Tacoma Public Library, Richards Collection.)

Cy Greenlaw (left) and cousin Earl Kuper were battery mates for the Tacoma Tigers of the Western International League during the 1946 and 1947 seasons. Greenlaw, a southpaw, won 25 games over those two seasons. Kuper hit .353 for the Tigers in 1946, and then in 1947 he led the league with a .389 average and finished his career with Tacoma as player-manger in 1948.

Red Harvel (left), manager of the Tacoma Tigers in 1947, chats with Les Patterson, a local scout for the Cincinnati Reds organization, while catcher Neil Clifford (second from the left) and pitcher Julian Morgan listen in. Patterson, who later scouted for the New York Yankees, was a catcher for the South Tacoma Tigers in 1915 that competed for the world championship.

TACOMA TIGERS - 1948

TOP ROW: Clay Huntington, *JORDAN'S Sportcaster* • Thomas Kipp • Cyrus Greenlaw • Henry Vallee • Joe Rossi • Dick Greco • Jim Gleason
Ray Fortier • Vince Lazor • Enoch Alexson, *General Manager*
MIDDLE ROW: Henry Sciarra • Larry Lee • Angelo Venturelli • Dan Perlmuter • Ken Clary • Buddy Lewis • Ray Tran • Vito De Vito
BOTTOM ROW: Giovanni Tomasi • Bernie Hargadon • Pat Steele • Jim Brillheart, *Manager* • Glenn Stetter • Terry Jordan, *Bat Boy*

The 1948 Tacoma Tigers were managed by Jim Brillheart and led by Dick Greco's 21 home runs and 126 RBIs, Glenn Stetter's .348 batting average, and catcher Joe Rossi, who went on to play professionally with Cincinnati.

George Nicholas, a gregarious pitcher for the Tigers in 1948, led the club with a 14-7 record and a miniscule earned run average of 2.42 as the team finished fourth in the Western International League.

Two days of rain forced Salem and Tacoma to open the 1949 season with a twin bill that saw the Senators defeat the Tigers, 7-3 and 2-1, before 4,535 fans. Player/manager Bob Johnson hit his 407th career home run in the sixth inning of the opening game. Mel Knezovich pitched the first game for the Tigers, and Bob Kerrigan pitched the second with the latter being halted after seven innings because the eighth would have taken the game past the 11:50 p.m. curfew.

Part of Opening Day Crowd 1949

The Wenatchee Chiefs defeated the Tigers 6-3 in game one of the second series of the season.

Bob Johnson enjoyed a 13-year major-league career—10 of those with the Philadelphia Athletics. The 1949 campaign was Johnson's 21st in professional baseball and was the only time in his career as a manager. The Tigers finished seventh with a 63-88 record.

In 1949, at the age of 43, manager Bob Johnson hit .326 for the Tigers; played first, third, and in the outfield for the club; and also took to the mound, where he appeared in 27 games and was 5-7 in 99 innings.

BACK ROW (Left to Right) – DON CARTER – RON GIFFORD – RED FISCHER – HUNK ANDERSON – KEITH BOWMAN – MEL KNEZOVICH – VINCE LAZOR – BOB KERRIGAN
MIDDLE ROW – FRANK GILLIHAN – JIM DALTON – DICK WENNER – SOL ISRAEL – DICK GRECO – TOM KIPP – WIMPY QUINN – CLAY HUNTINGTON – DAVE NADEAU
FRONT ROW – ORIN SNYDER – BILL SHEETS – MIKE CATRON – JIM BRILLHEART – GIL LOUST – BOB DAWSON – JOSE D. BACHE

The Tigers of 1950 completed the season with a 90-58 record, losing the league title to the Yakima Bears by one game. Glenn Stetter and Dick Greco were not only Tacoma's top hitters but also were first and second in the entire league with batting averages of .369 and .360, respectively. Bob Kerrigan was the workhorse of the pitching staff with a league-leading 26-7 record.

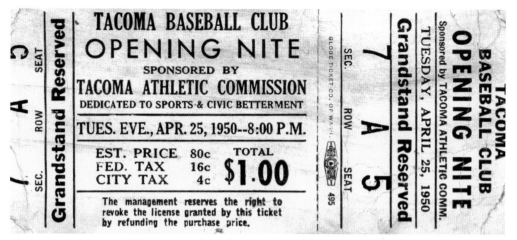

The season opener in 1950, sponsored by the Tacoma Athletic Commission, saw the Tigers take on the Spokane Indians and beat them 5-2 behind the pitching of Bob Kerrigan. Dick Greco had three singles in the game, but it was the double by Wimpy Quinn and two singles by Bill Sheets that did most of the damage.

All Tacoma Tigers road and home games were aired over KMO Radio and sponsored by Columbia Breweries. Clay Huntington, interviewing manager Jim Brillheart, was starting his fifth season doing the play-by-play with Bob Field doing the color.

Outfielder Dick Greco met Evelyn Moore at a restaurant in Victoria while on a spring road trip and got her number before leaving. They met up again five weeks later when the Tigers returned. Evelyn started listening to the games, and while in the clubhouse before a game, broadcaster Clay Huntington got news that Dick was marrying a girl from Victoria, so he announced that on the radio. Evelyn heard it, but since Dick had not asked her yet, the news came as a bit of a surprise. When Dick got back into town, she told him that she had listened to the broadcast and wanted to know if he had anything to ask her. He said, "Well, what do you think?" Evelyn said yes, and at the team's request they were married at Tiger Park on August 24, 1950.

TACOMA TIGERS - 1951

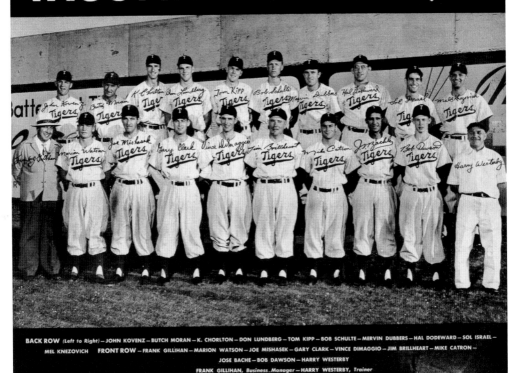

BACK ROW (Left to Right)—JOHN KOVENZ—BUTCH MORAN—K. CHORLTON—DON LUNDBERG—TOM KIPP—BOB SCHULTE—MERVIN DUBBERS—HAL DODEWARD—SOL ISRAEL—
MEL KNEZOVICH   FRONT ROW—FRANK GILLIHAN—MARION WATSON—JOE MISHASEK—GARY CLARK—VINCE DIMAGGIO—JIM BRILLHEART—MIKE CATRON—
JOSE BACHE—BOB DAWSON—HARRY WESTERBY
FRANK GILLIHAN, Business Manager—HARRY WESTERBY, Trainer

The 1951 Tigers were led by former Seattle Rainier outfielder K. Chorlton, who hit .343 and had 36 stolen bases in 93 games.

Jose Bache's professional career in baseball began in 1950 with the Tacoma Tigers when he arrived from Vera Cruz, Mexico, at age 27. A slick-fielding shortstop, Bache hit .275 for the Tigers in 1951.

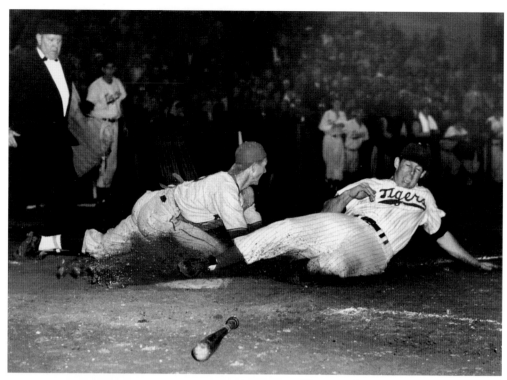

Umpire Clarence Stave calls Dick Greco out at home in a close play at Tiger Park.

Vince DiMaggio (left) was picked up at the airport by business manager Frank Gillihan, who lured him to the West Coast to finish out his career at the age of 38. Older brother of Joe and Dom, Vince played in the outfield for Tacoma and hit .225 in 74 games.

FASTPITCH SOFTBALL
1943–1974

Fastpitch softball came on the scene in 1938 with the sponsorship of the Tacoma Elks Club, and good recruiting in subsequent seasons enabled the Elks to remain one of the most highly competitive clubs well into the 1950s.

In the 1940s, softball became part of the war effort, with numerous businesses sponsoring teams as a way to enhance the home-front morale. The Tacoma Teamsters became the first Northwest entry to participate in the World Tournament, and although the club lost both games in Detroit it would not be a Tacoma team's last national appearance.

Uncle Sam must be credited with an assist for that success, since several Fort Lewis servicemen and another in the Coast Guard proved to be among the nation's elite fastpitch hurlers. Woodrow Red, Hal Blumke, Kermit Lynch, and Bob McCarty became the new pitching heroes of Tacoma and Pierce County. For several years they dominated the local softball scene and gave the area a regular taste of state, regional, and national play.

In 1945, the Stores-Machinists of Tacoma played in the World Softball Tournament in Cleveland, Ohio, where they finished third. The Tacoma Elks Club's softball domination was subsequently replaced by the Irwin-Jones Dodgers team that placed second in the World Tournament in Bridgeport, Connecticut, in 1952.

The final national tournament appearance belonged to Manke and Sons, who qualified for nationals in 1974 in Clearwater, Florida, by defeating perennial national powerhouse Pay 'n Pak of Seattle.

It was not until 1945 that women's teams sprouted up on a regular basis, such as Lincoln Electric of Tacoma and the Sumner Athletic Club. Coached by Bob Huegel, the Lincoln squad won the Washington state crown in 1945 and 1946 and then had to contend with a tough Sumner AC club winning several state titles of their own.

Other outstanding entries were the Tacoma Fuelerettes, coached initially by Frank Cey (whose son Ron would go on to enjoy a superlative major-league career), and Pacific Mutual Fuels.

The Hollywood Boat and Motor team of the early 1950s brought new meaning to the words "travel team" as they played throughout Washington, Oregon, Idaho, and Canada. Featuring Louise Mazzuca, a 14-year-old pitching phenom, the team helped increase the awareness of the sport by taking it to another level. Mazzuca, however, was in a class of her own, indicative of her induction into the Amateur Softball Association's National Hall of Fame in 2007.

In 1938, the Tacoma Elks club sponsored their first ever fastpitch team that competed in the Pro-Service-Vets League consisting of the Elks, the Bank of California, the Young Men's Business Club, the Red Men, the Knights of Columbus, and the Active Club. Managed by John Rappin (back row, center), the team wore uniforms consisting of long purple pants and shirts with the Elks emblem on the front.

By the time the 1940 season rolled around, the Elks team had recruited some of the better players in Tacoma; with fielding a better team, they also wore more conventional uniforms. With Charlie Green at the helm, the Elks Club defeated Johnson Paint to win the City League Championship. From left to right are (first row) Ted Iversen, Bill Wieking, Hank Peters, Bob McKinnell, Dick Savory, Reggie Johnson, and Dick Dexter; (second row) Charlie Green, Hal Deering, Bob Jepsen, Jerry Turner, Bill Jepsen, Dalton Thorne, Walt Olson, and Jack Nash.

The powerful Teamsters softball team of 1942 was the City League champion, and the roster included, from left to right, (first row) Frank Pavolka (first), John Hansler (third), and manager Bob Heugel (fourth); (second row) Tom Cross (second), Heinie Hademan (third), and Frank Morrone (sixth).

The 1943 Tacoma Teamsters defeated Kauffman Buick of Spokane 9-3 to win the Washington State Softball Championship behind the four-hit pitching of Woodrow Red. George Roket led the Teamsters at the plate with five hits and was named to the all-state team along with Red, catcher Hype Jensen, second baseman Bill Ruehle, and short fielder Bob Huegel. Manager Clyde Olson then took the club to the World Tournament in Detroit, Michigan, but they lost a pair of 2-1 games to Cincinnati, Ohio, and Kodak Park of Rochester, New York. It would not be a Tacoma team's last appearance at the "worlds."

The Eagles and Elks battled for City Softball League supremacy in 1943 with Woodrow Red (first row, center) on the mound for the Teamsters, while Bob Frankosky and Bill Ruehle shared mound duties for the Elks Club. The Eagles finished the season with a 26-4 record.

Tacoma's Coast Guard team compiled a 67-4 record during the 1944 season. From left to right are (first row) Robert Dowd, Walter Augland, Forest Lacy, Nat Moya, Elmer Litterell, Al Switzer, and Commanding Officer L. M. Archambeau; (second row) manager Chief Don Rippetoe, Al Cooke, Hubert Smith, Woodrow Red, Bill Sullivan, Arnold Baker, Paul Simpson, and Art Lewis.

Woodrow Red, stationed in the Coast Guard in Tacoma, had pitched his Arkansas team to state and regional championships in both 1941 and 1942 and would return to his home state to toss many more shutouts as one of the nation's premier hurlers.

John Rockway was one of Tacoma's finest fastpitch softball hurlers in the early 1940s when the sport was just on the rise. During his career he pitched for Seaview Tavern, Clothiers, and the Teamsters. Rockway later became the first Metro Tacoma Softball commissioner and was instrumental in the growth of fastpitch and slowpitch in Pierce County.

Behind the pitching of Hal Blumke and Kermit Lynch, the 1945 Stores-Machinists team won their first three games in the 13th-annual World Softball Tournament in Cleveland, Ohio. The team dropped their next two to finish third in the world championships. From left to right are (first row) Kermit Lynch, Bob McCarthy, and Harold Blumke; (second row) Hal Holcomb, Paul Larson, manager Clyde Olson, George Roket, and John Hudson; (third row) Private George Naka, George Robinson, Chuck McMillan, John Carbone, Jim Stores, and Vern From; missing from the shot are Earl Mahnkey, Les Holtmeyer, and Al Hernandez.

To honor a Stadium High School classmate killed in the war, Dick and George Pease formed a team and named it the Wes Hudson Athletic Club to honor their neighborhood friend. From left to right are (first row) Bud Thomsen, Stan Langlow, Lyle Kasbob, Will Gee, Chet Dyer, and George Pease; (second row) Dick Brown, Bob Lewis, Dick Burrows, scorekeeper Sylvia Thomsen, Dick Pease, Harold Campbell, and Lee Irwin.

The Elks Club of Tacoma was crowned City League champions in 1948. Vern From was a slugging catcher and brought leadership to the team from his years with Stores-Machinists, while Art Lewis was regarded as the best "hot corner" player in the state. Bob Frankosky was an imposing six-foot-four-inch windmill pitcher who baffled hitters, and Les Holtmeyer was a speedy outfielder who had been named to four state all-star teams earlier in his career. From left to right are (first row) Al Fawcett, Jim Martin, Bob Woods, Holtmeyer, and Bill Ruehle; (second row) From, Lewis, Henry Michalowski, and Alex Watt; (third row) Rudy Filion, Joey Johns, Frankosky, Tom Grzesiou, and Harry Corbin.

Whylie's Cafeman placed second in the 1950 state tournament, advancing to regional competition where they took fourth. From left to right are (first row) Coit Emerson, Dean Pitsch, Frank Whylie, Bob Zurfluh, R. Baker, and Glenn Collins; (second row) Bob Brahm, J. Kent, Bob Woods, Tex Vaughn, and B. Hart; (third row) Frank Davies, Ham Rush, Don Zurfluh, Bill Dunham, and D. McGinnis.

Just as servicemen added luster to the county softball ranks in the 1940s, the Tacoma Rockets hockey team brought a new wave of stellar softball talent to the "City of Destiny" in the 1950s. Doug Adam, Alex Watt, Joey Johns, Dick Milford, Rudy Filion, and Doug Stevenson all began to play locally. Adam and Watt joined Milford and Johns on the Irwin-Jones team of 1951, and a dynasty appeared to be in the making. Along with pitcher Lloyd Blanusa, the Dodgers dominated the local scene. Adam, a 1951 state tournament all-star, was a team leader and fine shortstop. Watt was one of the best "on-base" leadoff hitters in the game, while Milford caught Johns, making up one of the better batteries in the area. From left to right are (first row) Wally Brebner, Ples Irwin, Adam, and Vern Martineau; (second row) Johns, Milford, unidentified, Jack Hermsen, Bob Gunderson, Bob Frankosky, Watt, unidentified, and Lloyd Blanusa.

The Irwin-Jones Dodgers participated in the World Amateur Softball Association Tournament in Bridgeport, Connecticut, in 1952 and brought back second-place hardware for their efforts, losing to Dow Chemical of Midland, Michigan, 3-2, in the finale. From left to right are (first row) Dick Milford, Vern Martineau, Bob Gunderson, Ples Irwin, Wally Brebner, Bill Bridges, and Doug Adam; (second row) unidentified, Lloyd Blanusa, Doug Stromberg, Alex Watt, Bob Frankosky, Joey Johns, and Jack Hermsen.

FASTPITCH SOFTBALL: 1943–1974

Wood Realty represented the Tacoma area at the regional fastpitch tournament in Caldwell, Idaho, in 1955 after being crowned champions of the Northwest League. The Realtors were comprised of several former Dodgers players and two young pitchers who would star for years to come: Gene "Chico" Thayer and Dick Yohn. In addition, first baseman George Karpach was selected to the regional all-star team for the first time in his career. From left to right are (first row) Dick Webster, Wally Brebner, Bill Bellamy, Jack Hutchinson, and Jack Hermsen; (second row) Frank Davies, Karpach, Vern Martineau, Vic Martineau, and Dick Yohn; (third row) Bob Wood, Gordy Bendick, Fran Luhtala, Larry Slovek, and Butch Corbin; the batboy is unidentified.

A multi-sport athlete at Bellarmine Prep and Seattle University, George Karpach excelled in fastpitch from 1952 to 1973. Karpach was a Northwest Regional All-Star first baseman five times and played in four national tournaments, including with the Irwin-Jones Dodgers in 1952. He was player/manager for the Tacoma Athletics and Clearview Nursing Home and is a member of the Northwest Regional Softball Hall of Fame.

Jack Hermsen (sliding) was a mainstay on the Irwin-Jones Dodgers teams from 1951 to 1953 before moving on to play for the Wood Realty Ramblers in 1955 and 1956 and with Spring Air Mattress in 1957. (Jack Hermsen family.)

The 1966 Clearview Nursing Home fastpitch team won the Portland Rose Festival Championship with Chico Thayer and George Karpach leading the way. From left to right are (first row) Jay Beach, Dale Kruger, Andy Munro (sponsor), Lou Rickenbacker, Don Anderle, and Thayer; (second row) Joe Johnson, Don Rhodus, Frank Davies, Karpach, Bob Sonneman, Bill Winter, Ron Fawcett, and Warren Williams.

Women's fastpitch emerged on the scene in 1940 with the Tacoma Tigerettes and outfielder Gertrude Wilhelmsen, a discus and javelin competitor on the 1936 U.S. Olympic team in Berlin, leading the way. In 1945 and 1946, league champion Lincoln Electric, spotlighting standout pitcher Teddy Davis, went on to win state championships under coach Bob Huegel. From left to right are (first row) Margaret Heinrick, Patty Smith, Teddy Davis, Audrey Vaughn, and Bobby Huegel; (second row) Maureen MacLaughlin, Katy Vaughn, Peggy Moran Ruehle, Betty Keffler, and Agnes Hulscher; (third row) Marian Ricono, Betty Rowan, Jackie Church Pagni, Bebe Blake, C. Long, and coach Bob Huegel.

Margaret Heinrick started playing fastpitch at the age of 13 with the strong Lincoln Electric team and then played for the Sumner Athletic Club Maids in 1948 and 1949, winning the Washington State Softball Championship in the second year with the team. Maggie played every position on the diamond, including pitcher and catcher. As a 14 year-old, Maggie pitched against the Phoenix Queens and Her Court, one of the premier traveling teams in the country. She finished her fastpitch career with the Hollywood Boat & Motor team before moving on to play for the Cage Tavern, the first slowpitch team to qualify for nationals in Pierce County.

The Midland Tigers finished fourth in the state tournament in 1946, led by catcher and all-tournament selection Esther Deuel. Both Deuel and pitcher Barbara Taylor were honored for their all-around play, and for most of the players it was the start of a fastpitch career that would carry into the 1950s. From left to right are (first row) Patsy Hankinson, Louise Baskett, Maxine Raner, Pat Buffum, and Norma Buffum; (second row) manager Bob Doyle, treasurer Mrs. L. Ames, coach John Deuel, Barbara Taylor, Grace Sawtelle, Patsy Strachan, Janice Moore, Dorothy Sweet, Esther Deuel, and Tommy Hankinson.

Rufus "Boots" Christian, owner of Pacific Mutual Fuels, sponsored the Tacoma Fuelerettes in 1949, and 23-year-old Frank Cey coached them. Despite playing for the Midland Tigers several years earlier, the team was still inexperienced when it came to the fundamentals of the game. From left to right are (first row) Marjorie Johnson, Shirley Johnson, Dorothy Anderson, Dee Sagmiller, and Joyce Jones Wolf; (second row) Esther Deuel, Donna Brown, Patsy Hankinson, Ruth Canonica, and Virginia Penhale; (third row) Pat Strachan Stavig, Dorothy Miskar, Jueline Smith, Peggy Parsons, Louise Baskett, and coach Frank Cey.

Three of the top players for Pacific Mutual Fuels were Dorothy Miskar (left), Pat Strachan (center), and Dee Sagmiller. According to Coach Cey, "If I had to pick one person as the team leader it would have to be our catcher, Dorothy Miskar. She was a real workhorse. She was like a locomotive behind the plate—ain't nobody moving her out! She was a little older than the rest of the girls, and I think they looked up to her because of her experience and work ethic. Pat was a big, strong, versatile player for us. She was intimidating when she toed the mound, and I knew that I could bring her in the middle of a tough spot and she'd find a way to get us out of the jam. Dee was as fluid and confident of a player as one could want. She was strong for her stature, and she made everything look easy."

The Sumner Athletic Club Maids were state runners-up in 1946, competed in the state tournament in 1947 and 1948, and were crowned champions in 1949 behind pitcher Ann Kauzlarich and catcher Dora Deitz LaFaive, who were named to the all-star team. From left to right are (first row) Gloria Thoren Malley, Kate McHugh, Kauzlarich, LaFaive, Margaret Heinrick, and Doris Wanberg; (second row) manager Oliver Malley, Helen Thoren Jansen, Shirley Soggie, Frieda Schoenbachler Bostwick, Dorothy Cottrell, Dolores Benjamin, and coach Bob Chaplin.

Pacific Mutual Fuel, coached by Bill Stavig, won the 1951 Pierce County Women's Softball title with a 15-1 record, earning entry into the regional tournament in Richland. Shirley Soggie was named to the regional all-star team. From left to right are (first row) Donna Brown, Dorothy Anderson, Shirley Soggie, and Joyce Jones Wolf; (second row) Katy McHugh, Patsy Strachan Stavig, Ellen Schmidt; (third row) Delores Benjamin, Gloria Thoren Malley, Mary Jane Cooper Bramman, coach Bill Stavig, Patsy Hankinson, Sue Kauth, and Margaret Heinrick.

Hollywood Boat & Motor, sponsored by Harry Esborg and led by player/coach Margaret Zepeda, burst on the scene in 1956. Zepeda's team played locally and in the Northwest Women's Major League. Zepeda recruited some of the top players from the local leagues, including Louise Mazzuca, and "the Queens" became a major attraction. The club hosted a team featuring Charlotte Armstrong, who could throw from the pitcher's rubber, second base, or from center field and remain virtually unhittable. Team members are, from left to right, sponsor Harry Esborg, Margaret Zepeda, Joyce Jones Wolf, Sandy Molzan, Esther Deuel, unidentified, Jan Chase, Louise Mazzuca, Carol Schnuringer Boyer, unidentified, Alayne Butterfield, Gloria Longo, and coach Carl Benson; the woman kneeling is unidentified.

An avid softball player, Margaret Zepeda came to Tacoma in 1954, met Harry Esborg, owner and operator of Hollywood Boat and Motor, and sold him on the idea of sponsoring a women's softball team. Gathering players from local recreational teams, Zepeda—coach, team organizer, and top-level third baseman—put together a very competitive squad. After returning to Texas in 1957, Zepeda enjoyed a distinguished 28-year career as a coach of the Houston Comets, amassing the most coaching victories in Texas fastpitch history.

Joyce Jones Wolf joined the Pacific Mutual Fuels team at age 18 and played second base from 1948 to 1951. She also played for the Tacoma Orphans and the Rustlers and Hustlers before joining the Hollywood Boat and Motor team for three seasons. Joyce became the most successful women's slowpitch coach in Tacoma-Pierce County history, where during a three-year period her teams had a record of 151-19 and won 19 of 22 tournaments in which they were considered "the" team to beat throughout Washington and Oregon.

The Hollywood Boat Queens noticed that many of their opponents were donning uniforms made of a material with a satin feel, the kind worn in the movie A League of Their Own. Owner Harry Esborg, not wanting to shortchange his team, outfitted his players in the latest in fastpitch fashion. From left to right are (first row) Sandy Molzan, Phyllis Brady, Dee Sagmiller, Patsy Hankinson, two unidentified; (second row) Margaret Heinrick, two unidentified, Harry Esborg, Sue Kauth, Shirley Harris, and Marilyn Winski.

Louise Mazzucca began playing on park league teams at age 11 and played for Tacoma's Hollywood Boat Club from 1954 to 1957. In her career, Mazzuca, a 1958 Stadium High graduate, hurled 35 no-hitters and nine perfect games. Three of her no-hitters came in the 1960 ASA Women's Major Fastpitch National Championship as she compiled a 4-2 record, fanning 75 batters. Her most impressive feat was in the 1964 regional tournament, when she pitched a seven-inning game that her team won, took a 20 minute rest, and then pitched against Joan Joyce and the Orange, California, team. This epic classic between two of the greatest pitchers in the world lasted 29 innings before Orange won, 1-0. In the space of one night, Mazzuca pitched a total of 36 consecutive innings. In 2007, Louise was enshrined in the ASA National Softball Hall of Fame, only the second female from the state of Washington to receive this honor.

Lowell Nelson managed a 1974 Manke & Sons squad that advanced to the ASA National Tournament after defeating powerful Pay 'n Pak of Seattle to win the Northwest Regional title. Manke & Sons was the first Pierce County team to play in a national tournament since the Irwin-Jones Dodgers team of 1952. During a three-season run, Nelson directed the team to three straight Pierce County regional titles with key players Chico Thayer, Jay Beach, Keith Bauer, Bill Boyer, Darron Nelson, Lloyd Glasoe, Ron Vandegrift, and Henry Jarvits leading the charge.

In 1980, Cheney Stadium was the site of the World Softball Tournament with 14 teams from around the world competing in the nine-day event. The U.S. squad claimed the title with a 3-0 win over Canada in the nine-inning finale.

THE PACIFIC
COAST LEAGUE
1960–2010

Tacoma joined the Pacific Coast League in 1904 following acquisition of the Sacramento franchise. Under manager Mike Fisher, the Tigers proceeded to win the first Pacific Coast League title in Tacoma history. Unfortunately it was a short existence in the PCL for the Tigers, as they moved back to Sacramento after the first half of the 1905 season due to financial reasons.

Pacific Coast League baseball returned to the City of Destiny in 1960, when the San Francisco Giants moved their Triple-A affiliate to Tacoma from Phoenix. The efforts were initiated by Phoenix general manger W. D. "Rosy" Ryan and spearheaded locally by Clay Huntington of the Tacoma Athletic Commission, Mayor Ben Hanson, community leader Morley Brotman, and Pierce County Commissioner Harry Sprinker, but it was the commitment by local philanthropist and sportsman Ben Cheney to construct a stadium by opening day that sealed the deal.

Tacoma has enjoyed baseball for 50 years at Cheney Stadium, and the city owns the longest continual service streak in the Pacific Coast League as a result. During this time, the team has been known as the Giants (1960–1965), Cubs (1966–1971), Twins (1972–1977), Yankees (1978), Tugs (1979), Tigers (1980–1994), and Rainiers (1995–2010).

Since the 1904 PCL title, Tacoma has won championship crowns as the Giants in 1961, the Cubs in 1969, the Yankees in 1978, and the Rainiers in 2001 and 2010. They have also witnessed a number of outstanding performances from the likes of Juan Marichal, Gaylord Perry, Matty Alou, Burt Hooten, Tom Kelly, Bill Campbell, Jose Canseco, Mark McGwire, Walt Weiss, Alex Rodriguez, and Felix Hernandez.

Players such as Dustin Ackley, Greg Hallman, and Michael Pineda are destined for future stardom, and with a $30-million remodeled Cheney Stadium planned for opening day 2011, the future of baseball in Tacoma-Pierce County indeed looks "Rosy."

Motivated by lumber magnate Ben Cheney, who donated $100,000, Tacoma built Cheney Stadium, which still serves as the team's home. Known as the "100-day wonder," workers took only three months and 14 days to complete construction in time for the April 16, 1960, opening game between the Tacoma Giants and the Portland Beavers. The new field featured light standards and wooden seats from Seal Stadium, which had been the longtime home of San Francisco's Coast League team. A life-size, bronze statue of Ben Cheney watching a game was unveiled in the reserved seating section at Cheney Stadium on April 6, 1995.

PROPOSED GRANDSTAND · TACOMA-PIERCE COUNTY BASEBALL PARK ~~ AS SUBMITTED BY BEN. B. CHENEY

When the Tacoma City Council and Pierce County Commissioners approved Ben Cheney's bid of $840,000, things moved fast at the chosen site of the Snake Lake area at South Twenty-fifth Street and Bantz Boulevard, and 14 weeks later the ballpark was ready for the cry of "play ball!" The original dimensions were 410 feet in center field and 330 feet down the line in left and right fields.

After 14 years as voice of the Louisville Colonels of the American Association starting in 1938, Don Hill was signed as the radio announcer for Tacoma Giants games. Curt Gowdy tipped Hill off about the job, and when Don called Rosy Ryan about the job, Ryan remembered him from a visit his Minneapolis Millers team made to Louisville on Radio Appreciation Night that drew a crowd of 18,000. In those days, the visiting team took 22¢ a head, and Ryan was impressed and never forgot it. Don's signature call was, "How about that, Giants fans?"

Fort Lewis gave nature a hand in drying out the field at Cheney Stadium in preparation for the Pacific Coast League home opener on April 16, 1960. The original opening day had to be postponed for two days due to a 59 mile-per-hour spring storm, massive rains, and low temperatures. The smoke is from a napalm fire set on the infield dirt. Soldiers were using portable Herman Nelson heaters to help dry the turf.

Following two days of heavy rain, the Tacoma Giants played their first Pacific Coast League game in 55 years and, with Eddie Fisher on the mound, dropped a 7-2 decision to the Portland Beavers. In the nightcap of the day-night twin bill, the Giants bounced back behind the rookie debut of Juan Marichal. The doubleheader drew 12,283 fans. The 1960 Tacoma Giants finished with an 81-73 record, which was good enough for second place. From left to right are (first row) ballboy Jerry Hicks, Ossie Alvarez, Benny Valenzuela, Matty Alou, Jose Pagan, and home team batboy Mark Wojahn; (second row) Harry McCarthy (kneeling), Danny O'Connell, Frank Reveira, Julio Navarro, Don Choate, Red Davis, Sal Taormina, Dom Zanni, and Dick Phillips; (third row) Leo "Doc" Hughes, Don Hill, Bob Farley, Marshall Renfroe, Clay Huntington, Bobby Prescott, Eddie Fisher, Bob Perry, Tom Haller, Dusty Rhodes, Verle Tiefenthaler, Juan Marichal, Sherman "Roadblock" Jones, Ramon Monzant, Jim Duffalo, Lew Matlin, Rosy Ryan, and Ben Cheney; missing from the image is team physician Dr. Sam Adams.

Red Davis managed the Tacoma Giants from 1960 to 1962 and amassed a 259-203 win-loss record during his three years in Tacoma. A legendary minor-league manager for 27 seasons, the Giants finished second, first, and third in Red's three seasons at the helm of the Giants.

Juan Marichal only played in 18 games for the 1960 Tacoma Giants but parlayed a successful season into a mid-season promotion to the San Francisco Giants and never looked back on the way to a Hall of Fame career. The 22-year-old started the second game of an opening-day doubleheader against the Portland Beavers and whitewashed the visitors 11-0. While in Tacoma the "Dominican Dandy" finished with an 11-5 record, 12 complete games, and a 3.11 ERA. In 139 innings as pitcher, he tallied 121 strikeouts while issuing only 39 walks. In 1984, he was named to Tacoma's All-Time Team.

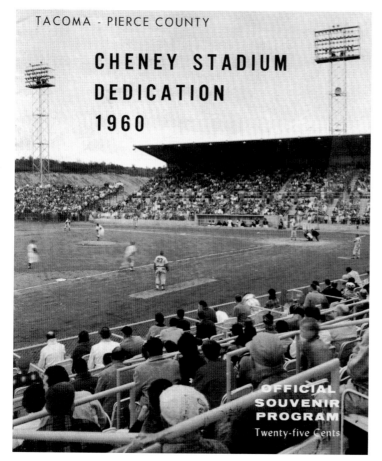

TACOMA - PIERCE COUNTY

CHENEY STADIUM
DEDICATION
1960

OFFICIAL
SOUVENIR
PROGRAM
Twenty-five Cents

Cheney Stadium was dedicated on June 16, 1960, and those recognized for bringing the Giants franchise to Tacoma included Ben Cheney; Harry Sprinker, chairman of the board of Pierce County Commissioners; Clay Huntington, chairman of the State Sports Council and a Tacoma Athletic Commission founding member; Mayor Ben Hanson; and sportswriters Dan Walton and Ed Honeywell.

When Cheney Stadium opened, it included 1,320 box seats, 764 grandstand reserve seats, 3,326 general admission seats, and 2,600 bleacher seats for a total of 8,010. Over 51 years, the teams have played in front of over 12 million fans. Behind the right-field wall was a vacant hillside that filled up quickly when the Giants were in town. Known as Tightwad Hill, youngsters chased down baseballs during batting practice, and the ball club would send popcorn, hotdog, and soda pop vendors to hawk their wares as well.

Dusty Rhodes enjoyed a successful debut with the Tacoma Giants, going 2-4 in both games of the 1960 opening-day doubleheader as the T-Giants earned a split with the Portland Beavers. A 1954 World Series hero for the New York Giants, Dusty played in Tacoma from 1960 to 1962 and led the club with 23 round-trippers in the inaugural season. A colorful character and full of stories, Dusty left a lasting impression when he decided to "hang 'em up," as he literally nailed his cleats to the clubhouse ceiling in Cheney Stadium upon his retirement at the end of the 1962 season.

General manager W. D. "Rosy" Ryan displays the Triple-A National Association Attendance Derby trophy won by the Tacoma Giants in 1960. The club attracted 270,024 fans, as PCL baseball returned to the City of Destiny.

Red Davis led the 1961 Giants to the Pacific Coast League crown with a 97-57 record, the best record in Tacoma's modern history. Many baseball historians consider this club to be one of the greatest minor-league teams ever assembled. Gaylord Perry and Ron Herbel led the pitching staff with 16 victories each.

Your 1961 Tacoma Giants — Don Hill — KTAC's "Voice of the Giants" — How About That Giant Fans!

Back Row, left to right—Jim Duffalo, RHP; Bob Perry, OF; John Orsino, C; Bill Hain, IF; Geo. Maranda, RHP; Bud Byerly, Coach-RHP; Rafael Alomar, OF; "Dusty" Rhodes, LF; Leo Hughes, Trainer. **Middle Row**—Gaylord Perry, RHP; Ray Daviault, RHP; Lynn Lovenguth, RHP; Chuck Hiller, IF; John "Red" Davis, Manager; Ron Herbel, RHP; Dom Zanni, RHP; Verle Tiefenthaler, RHP; Eddie Fisher, RHP. **Front Row**—John Goetz, RHP; Gil Garrido, SS; Frank Reveira, Catcher; Richard Keely, Bat boy; Greg Hume, Bat boy; Jerry Hicks, Ball boy; Manny Mota, OF; Bob Farley, OF. Unavailable when picture was taken were Tom Haller, Catcher, and Dick Phillips, Utility.

Dick Phillips is the only Tacoma player to ever win a league MVP award as the 1961 Giants won their first PCL title. Phillips batted .264 with 16 home runs and a team-leading 98 RBIs while walking 94 times with only 55 strikeouts. He played every infield and outfield position and was a member of the all-star team.

Gil Garrido led shortstops in fielding percentage from 1961 to 1964 and won two Rawlings Silver Glove awards. Only 19 years old when he joined the Giants in 1961, Garrido was a fixture at shortstop for the next five seasons. He was a member of three all-star teams, holds the franchise record for most sacrifice hits in a season with 18, and is the all-time career leader for games played (691), at-bats (2651), runs scored (338), hits (663), total bases (782), and triples (24). Making the presentation are PCL president Dewey Soriano (left) and Rawlings's Oscar Roettger.

Gaylord Perry threw 219 innings as a workhorse for the pennant-winning Giants in 1961, finishing with a 16-10 record and leading the league with a 2.48 ERA. Gaylord was selected as one of the four starting pitchers to Tacoma's all-time PCL team in 1984. Perry, who came all the way from his peanut farm in North Carolina to participate in the festivities, commented, "They think these days that owners and general managers are tough. They should have known Rosy Ryan. I came here in 1960 and pitched one inning. I gave up one home run in that inning, and I was on my way back to Double-A ball. That's how tough Rosy was!"

John Pregenzer was an imposing sight at six feet, five inches as he trudged in from the bullpen to snuff out a rally, which he did frequently. During his three seasons in Tacoma, "Big John" compiled a 17-11 record and totaled 208 strikeouts in 233 innings of work. During his stay with the San Francisco Giants, the John Pregenzer Fan Club was formed, complete with T-shirts, newsletters, and membership cards for the 8,000-strong organization.

Dick Estelle, a southpaw pitcher, tossed two no-hitters as a Tacoma Giant. He beat the Denver Bears 2-0 in nine innings on June 22, 1964, and then followed that up on May 11, 1965, with a 6-0 shutout against the Hawaii Islanders. Dick LeMay threw the first no-hitter in Tacoma Giants history in 1962, followed by Jerry Thomas's seven-inning gem against Denver in 1963.

In anticipation of the opening game of the 1967 Pacific Coast League season, Tacoma Cubs fans decided to get a jump on purchasing their season tickets with general manager Bobby Adams manning the ticket booth. After renewing his order for 10 box seats, Ben Cheney donned popcorn vender's paraphernalia to help add to the atmosphere. Waiting in line are, from left to right, Lorraine Higginbothem, John Radonich, Spec Osborne, Colonel James Stack, H. A. Mierow, J. R. Beatson, R. W. Beal, Pat Patterson, and Roy Nelson. Patterson was well known for his Donald Duck impersonations and sat in a field box seat next to the third base dugout and regaled the visiting team with his constant banter.

After a successful 15-year career in the major leagues, Whitey Lockman moved into the managerial ranks and was at the helm of the Tacoma Cubs from 1967 to 1970.

The 1969 Tacoma Cubs amassed an 86-60 record en route to the Pacific Coast League Championship under skipper Whitey Lockman. Lockman's record was the third best in the 51-year history of the Tacoma franchise behind the .590 mark (85-59) of Dan Rohn in 2001 with the Tacoma Rainiers and the all-time best of .630 (97-57) turned in by Red Davis in 1961 with the Tacoma Giants.

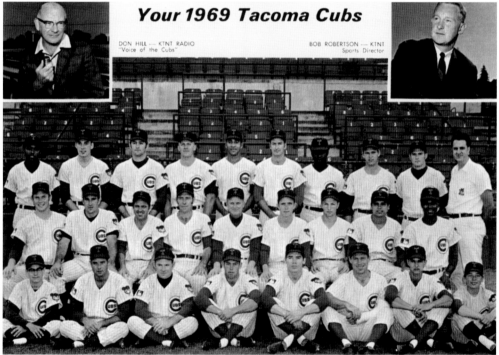

Front Row, left to right: Charles Spruck, Bat Boy; George Sherrod, RHP; Al Montreuil, IF; John Lung, IF; Vic LaRose, IF; Mike White, OF; Roger Metzger, SS; Bob Bianchi, Bat Boy. **Middle Row, left to right:** Jim Colborn, RHP; Jim Dunegan, OF; Ron Piche, RHP; Bob Tiefenauer, RHP; Whitey Lockman, Mgr.; Larry Gura, LHP; Rick Bladt, OF; George Pena. Utlity; Aaron Pointer, CF. **Back Row, left to right:** Chet Trail, IF; Darcy Fast, LHP; Archie Reynolds, RHP; Roe Skidmore, IB; John Hairston, C; Dick LeMay, LHP; Jim McMath, OF; Randy Bobb, C; Joe Decker, RHP; Gary Nicholson, Trainer.

Aaron Pointer joined the Tacoma Cubs in 1968 and helped them win the PCL crown the following season. Pointer is the last professional baseball player to hit .400 over an entire season, a feat he accomplished in 1961 when he hit .402 for Salisbury in the Western Carolina League. A fleet-footed outfielder, he was also a member of the All-Rookie lineup put on the field by the Houston Colt .45s on September 27, 1963, in the Astrodome that featured Joe Morgan, Jimmy Wynn, and Rusty Staub.

Joe Decker pitched for the Tacoma Cubs in 1968 and 1969 and was one of three pitchers on that championship squad to have 10 wins. He debuted with the Chicago Cubs the following month and spent nine seasons in the major leagues.

The Tacoma Cubs defeated Eugene, three games to two, to win the PCL title in 1969. Jim Colborn, the league leader with a 2.28 ERA, tossed five innings of shutout ball and Dick LeMay closed the door to preserve the 2-0 shutout in the finale played in Eugene before 6,135 fans. The players in front from left to right are (first row) Jim Dunegan, catcher Randy Bobb, Jim McMath (no. 2), Roe Skidmore, George Pena (no. 1), golfer and superfan Ken Still, and Archie Reynolds; above Reynolds is Dick LeMay, and in the upper left is Mike White.

When the Chicago Cubs moved the team to Wichita at the end of the 1971 season, rumors were that baseball would be lost forever in Tacoma. Enter Stan Naccarato who rounded up 20 investors within two days willing to put up $5,000 each to keep a team in Tacoma. A working agreement was finalized with Minnesota, and a six-year relationship with the club started with the 1972 Tacoma Twins. From left to right are (first row) unidentified batboy, Hal Haydel, Jerry Terrell, Ken Gill, John Gelnar, Tom Kelly, Bill Burback, Ezell Carter, and two unidentified batboys; (second row) Vic Albury, Mike Adams, Fred Rico, Rich Barnes, Mike Brooks, Bucky Guth, Dennis Saunders, and Rick Dempsey; (third row) Buck Chamberlain, Harry Warner, Jim Holt, unidentified, Jose Arcia, Steve Luebber, Cap Peterson, Mark Wiley, Ron Herbel, Glenn Ezell, Mike Derrick, and groundskeeper Scotty Ryan.

BASEBALL IN TACOMA-PIERCE COUNTY

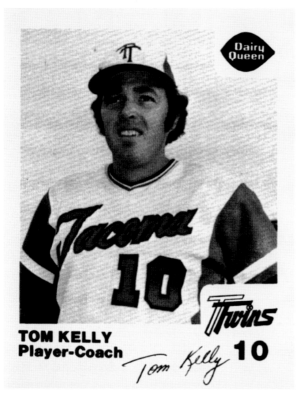

TOM KELLY
Player-Coach *Tom Kelly* **10**

Tom Kelly spent five years as a member of the Tacoma Twins—four as a player and in 1977 as a player/coach, where he shared managing duties with Del Wilbur. He is the all-time career leader in walks with 362 and ranks second all time in games played, at-bats, runs, hits, and home runs. Kelly went on to manage the Minnesota Twins for 16 years and won two World Series with the Twins. Kelly's teammate in 1973 was Charlie Manuel, winner of a World Series title in 2008 as manager of the Philadelphia Phillies.

Cal Ermer (right), manager of the Tacoma Twins in 1975, shortstop Jim Van Wyck (left), and second baseman Jerry Terrell lobby unsuccessfully with umpire Fred Brocklander. Van Wyck played for the Tacoma Twins from 1973 to 1977 and then worked in the Tacoma Yankees' front office in 1978. He then entered the film industry and has produced many films, including *The Babe*, *Lethal Weapon 4*, *Free Willy*, and *Dick Tracy*.

In 1975, professional golfer Ken Still signed a contract with the Tacoma Twins as a non-playing coach and was scheduled to be in uniform when not on the PGA Tour. An avid baseball fan, Still manned the first-base coaching box to open the 1975 season opener, a 5-3 Twins victory.

Stan Naccarato served as general manager of Tacoma's teams from 1972 to 1994. In 1975, he received The *Sporting News* Executive of the Year award, the "President's Trophy," and the Larry McPhail Promotional Trophy, emblematic of Tacoma's stature as number-one franchise in minor-league baseball. At that time, no one in the 77-year history of the national association had won all three major awards in the same year.

The path Art Popham followed took him from Kansas City A's batboy in 1966–1967 to public relations/promotions director for Charlie Finley's Oakland A's from 1970 through 1972 to the voice of the Tacoma Twins in 1976, a roll he filled through 1984. Art and wife Kathy are shown here with Jim "Catfish" Hunter (left) and Rollie Fingers (right) in 1972, pitchers for the A's and now enshrined in the Baseball Hall of Fame.

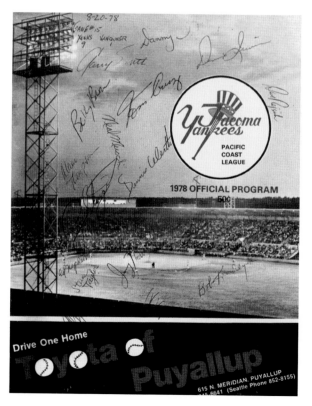

The Tacoma Yankees, managed by Mike Ferraro, were 80-57 in 1978 and were declared co-champions with Albuquerque when weather halted the championship series. It was Ferraro's second appearance in a Tacoma uniform; his last year as a player was in 1973 as a member of the Tacoma Twins.

Outfielder Dell Alston connects for a round-tripper in the home opener at Cheney Stadium on April 23, 1978, and the Tacoma Yankees defeated the San Jose Missions, 7-3, before a KMO Day crowd of 10,103. The Yankees went on to win 8 out of 10 games on their first home stand of the season. Alston led the club with a .348 batting average for the year. Hoyt Wilhelm, who enjoyed a 21-year Hall of Fame major-league career, signed on to serve as the pitching coach for the Tacoma Yankees. Roger Slagle, Bob Kammeyer, Jim Lysgaard, and Larry McCall combined for 45 of the team's 80 wins, and Jim Beattie tossed a seven-inning, 2-0 no-hitter against the Spokane Indians on July 9 as part of Wilhelm's pitching corps. McCall led the PCL with a 2.93 ERA.

In three seasons at the helm of the Tacoma Tigers, skipper Ed Nottle led the club to two Northern Division titles, and in 1981 Nottle was named Baseball America's Minor League Manager of the Year and Pacific Coast League Manager of the Year. While managing Tacoma, Ed once got tossed from a game, so he went back into the clubhouse and emerged wearing the Tiger mascot suit. Known as the "Singing Manager," Nottle recorded an album with the Oakland Symphony Orchestra. In 1984, he received the greatest recognition of his managerial career-selection as Tacoma's all-time manager.

Jim Nettles was a teammate of Tom Kelly and former Cy Young winner Mike McCormick on the Tacoma Twins team in 1973. He returned to play with the Tigers in 1981 before spending three seasons as the team's hitting coach. Jim and his brother Graig rank fifth all-time among brother combinations in home runs with a total of 406—Craig has 390 and Jim 16.

Slugging first baseman Kelvin Moore burst onto the scene in 1981 with a .329 batting average to go with his 31 home runs and 109 RBIs. Moore finished seventh and ninth on the career leaderboard for home runs and RBIs, respectively, in three seasons with the Tigers.

Gaylord Perry and Tom Haller were honored as members of Tacoma's All-Time All-Star Team on August 2, 1984, during special on-field ceremonies at Cheney Stadium. Team members included manager Ed Nottle, catcher Haller, first baseman Kelvin Moore, second baseman Tito Fuentes, third baseman Rick Renick, shortstop Gil Garrido, outfielders Matty Alou, Adrian Garrett, and Dusty Rhodes, designated hitter Mitchell Page, starting pitchers Juan Marichal, Perry, and Burt Hooton, and relief pitchers Eddie Fisher and John Pregenzer. The Most Popular Player was Tom Kelly. In front from left to right are Bob Robertson, Bill Hain, Pip Koehler, Perry, Haller, Piper Cheney, broadcaster Don Hill, and an unidentified man.

Bob Robertson, formerly the sports director at Channel 11 (KTNT and KSTW) when Tacoma Giants games were broadcast on television in the 1960s, was hired as the "voice of the Tigers" for the 1985 season following the retirement of Art Popham after nine seasons at the microphone.

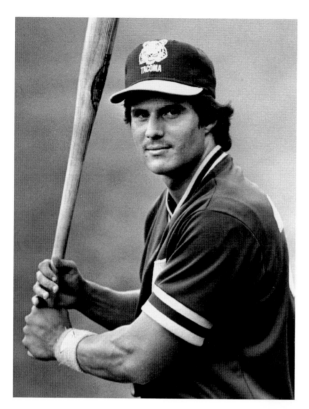

In 60 games for the Tigers in 1985, Jose Canseco hit .348 with 11 home runs and 47 RBIs. At age 21, his power was already being compared to that of Harmon Killebrew, Reggie Jackson, and Willie Stargell. Others said he was reminiscent of Orlando Cepeda as a young slugger, and some said that his power, strong arm, and speed were similar in many respects to Mickey Mantle.

While Jose Canseco was on his way to American League Rookie of the Year honors with the Oakland A's, the next slugger to come along was third baseman Mark McGwire, who blasted 13 home runs and 59 RBIs in 78 games with the 1986 Tigers. The following season he too earned Rookie of the Year accolades with the Athletics. Walt Weiss became the third Tiger in a row to win the honor in 1988.

Frank Colarusso, director of marketing in his first year with the Tigers in 1986, successfully convinced general manager Stan Naccarato to dress up like Uncle Sam to promote the upcoming July 3 game and fireworks show. The idea was to have a color ad in the *News Tribune* reading, "Uncle Stan wants YOU at Cheney Stadium." Needless to say, ticket sales went crazy, and by early in the week the game was sold out.

The 1992 Tacoma Tigers set an all-time, single-season attendance record, drawing 329,00 fans to Cheney Stadium in the franchise's 33rd year of operation. Frank Colarusso was named general manager, Kevin Kalal served as the public relations director, and Bob Christofferson was in the midst of a 20-year career as head groundskeeper at Cheney Stadium before he was hired in the same capacity for the Seattle Mariners.

Troy Neel became the first player in Tacoma's history to win the Pacific Coast League batting title after hitting .351 for the 1992 season. A left-handed, designated hitter/outfielder, Neel's .351 is the highest batting average in club history and broke the old mark of .333 set by Jim Holt with the Tacoma Twins in 1972. Neel led the Tigers in home runs, RBIs, hits, runs, doubles walks, slugging percentage, and on-base percentage and was the PCL's all-star designated hitter.

Scott Brosius played third base for the Tacoma Tigers from 1990 to 1993 and was traded by Oakland to the New York Yankees in 1998. Scott proceeded to bat .300 with 19 home runs and 98 RBIs, was selected to the all-star team, and was named the World Series MVP as the Yankees won the first of three consecutive championships.

The 1995 season was a new era for Tacoma baseball as the team adopted the nickname Rainiers after 15 years of being known as the Tigers. In 54 games, shortstop Alex Rodriguez hit .360 with 15 home runs and 44 RBIs. His performance earned him a promotion to the Seattle Mariners, and he never looked back. (Tacoma Rainiers Baseball Club.)

Ken Griffey Jr. made the only Triple-A appearance of his professional career on August 13, 1995, at a sun-splashed Cheney Stadium as a member of the Tacoma Rainiers. Sidelined for 11 weeks with a broken wrist, Griffey's day at the plate was recorded 1-3, 5-3, and a K, but that did not matter to the 7,268 spectators who were just happy to see him. (Michael Sage Photography.)

From left to right, outfielder Anthony Sanders, pitchers Todd Williams and Ryan Franklin, and outfielder Mike Neill throw out the first pitch at a Seattle Mariners game at Safeco field during the 2000 season. The occasion was to honor the four Rainiers players who were members of the U.S. Olympic baseball team. (Shanaman Sports Museum.)

On July 7, 2001, John Halama tossed the first nine-inning perfect game in the 99-year history of the Pacific Coast League, defeating the Calgary Cannons 6-0 on a 97-pitch perfect night. Halama had been sent down to the minors on June 29 to work on his mechanics, and in his first start he defeated Oklahoma City 4-1 on just four hits. He joined the Seattle Mariners as the player to be named in the 1998 trade that sent Randy Johnson to Houston. (Tacoma Rainiers Baseball Club.)

On July 3, 2001, Brett Tomko (right) tossed a no-hitter against Oklahoma City, defeating the hometown RedHawks 7-0. It was the first no-hitter by a Tacoma pitcher since Pat Wernig's no-no in 1991. Four days later, on July 7, John Halama (left) duplicated the feat, just the tenth no-hitter in Tacoma's history since 1960. Blake Berthol (center) caught both of the no-hitters.

Tacoma first baseman A. J. Zapp hit what was thought to be longest home run in the 45-year history of Cheney Stadium on September 1, 2004, against the visiting Sacramento Rivercats in a 7-4 loss. Zapp's solo home run in the third inning went over the 29-foot-high wall in center field—425 feet from home plate; the ball carried an estimated 505 feet. (Shanaman Sports Museum.)

Front row (right to left): Ryan Schutt (Head Groundskeeper), Rich Arneson (Visiting Clubhouse Manager), Kyle Piazza (Bullpen Catcher), Tal Edman (Batboy), Jeff Bopp (Clubhouse Manager), Kevin Kalal (Asst. General Manager), Mark Brennan (Strength/Conditioning Coach).
Second row: Rob Nodine (Trainer), Jeff Harris, Miguel Olivo, Ramon Santiago, Jamal Strong, Dan Rohn (Manager), Yuniesky Betancourt, Jeff Heaverlo, Chris Buglovsky.
Third row: Chris Snelling, Justin Leone, Ryan Christianson, Rich Dorman, Shin-Soo Choo, Hunter Brown, Aaron Rifkin, Jared Thomas.
Back row (standing): Felix Hernandez, Terry Pollreisz (Coach), Jorge Campillo, Masao Kida, George Sherrill, Jose Lopez, Abraham Nunez, Andrew Lorraine, Michael Bumstead, Sean Green, Cha-Seung Baek, Dave Lewis (General Manager), Rafael Chaves (Pitching Coach).

Sporting a 375-340 record as manager of the Tacoma Rainiers from 2001–2005, Dan Rohn became the first manager in Pacific Coast League history to be selected as the league's manager of the year three times. Rohn, an infielder with the Tacoma Tigers in 1987, skippered the club to the co-championship with New Orleans in 2001 when the playoff series was canceled in the aftermath of the terrorist actions of September 11.

Felix Hernandez pitched for the Tacoma Rainiers during the 2005 season and finished with a 9-4 win-loss record, recording 100 strikeouts and a 2.25 ERA. (Tacoma Rainiers Baseball Club.)

The Schlegel Sports Group completed purchase of Tacoma's baseball franchise from George and Sue Foster in time to take over the club for the start of the 2007 season. It was a banner year in 2010 during the franchise's 51st year of existence; the club set an all-time attendance record of 363,365 fans, and the team won the PCL Pacific Conference crown with a 5-4 series win over the Sacramento Rivercats in the semi-finals. The Rainiers then defeated the Memphis Redbirds in the championship round 3-0 for the Pacific Coast League title, the fifth in club history and the first outright crown since the 1969 Tacoma Cubs. Playing for the Triple-A championship, the Rainiers dropped a 12-6 decision to the Columbus Clippers. (Tacoma Rainiers Baseball Club.)

Four days after the final game was played in the original Cheney Stadium on September 6, a ground-breaking was held to commemorate the $30 million remodeling of the ballpark that is slated for completion in time for the April 15, 2011, home opener. Amenities include 16 luxury suites, the Summit Club on the top level that includes views of the ballpark and Mt. Rainier, new dugouts, left-field bleachers perched just above inset bullpens, a grass berm in right field where people can enjoy the game picnic style on a blanket, overall seating for close to 8,000 fans, and other amenities to enhance the experience. (Tacoma Rainiers Baseball Club.)

www.arcadiapublishing.com

Discover books about the town where you grew up, the cities where your friends and families live, the town where your parents met, or even that retirement spot you've been dreaming about. Our Web site provides history lovers with exclusive deals, advanced notification about new titles, e-mail alerts of author events, and much more.

Find Your Place in History.